BY THE SAME AUTHOR:

PLAYS VOLUME ONE (*Jenousia and Seven Impromptus*)
PLAYS VOLUME TWO (*The Satyr of La Villette, The Unknown General, Wide Open Spaces*)
THE WIND IN THE BRANCHES OF THE SASSAFRAS
THE CENTENARIAN (*A novel*)

OBALDIA

Two Women For One Ghost
The Baby-Sitter
The Jellyfishes' Banquet

PLAYS VOLUME THREE

Translated by Donald Watson

JOHN CALDER · LONDON
RIVERRUN PRESS · NEW YORK

First published in Great Britain 1982 by
John Calder (Publishers) Limited
18 Brewer Street London W1R 4AS

and in the USA 1982 by
Riverrun Press Inc
175 Fifth Avenue, New York 10010

Originally published in France 1973 as *René de Obaldia Théâtre V* by
Editions Bernard Grasset

842.914
Ob1P
139340

Jul 1986

BRITISH LIBRARY CATALOGUING IN PUBLICATION DATA
Obaldia, René de
    Obaldia plays.
    Vol. 3
    I. Title
    842'.914   PQ2629.B3

ISBN 0-7145-3559-1 paperback

Typeset in 9/10 point Press Roman by Gilbert Composing Services of
Leighton Buzzard, Beds, Great Britain.
Printed and bound in the Channel Islands
by the Guernsey Press Co. Ltd.

CONTENTS

wo Women for One Ghost 7

he Baby-Sitter 39

he Jellyfishes' Banquet 71

Characters

BRIGITTE

About forty. Elegant. Beneath her
protective clothing she has a body that
one would guess to be agreeably appetizing.
Her face, without being particularly pretty,
is comely. Something that catches the eye.
She is Pierre's wife.

VIVIANE

She could almost be a Brigitte. But a
slightly younger version; a bit more relaxed,
more athletic and liberated. Viviane, who
lives alone, works. She is divorced.
(Brigitte would like to work.) A rather
more 'open' character. A little less . . . She
is Pierre's mistress.
These two women, who never asked to be
born, at once arouse our sympathy. They
follow the deep-laid instincts of their
sex . . . which, needless to say, does not
fail to raise problems.

GHOST of PIERRE

Exactly like Pierre. Looks pretty square.
Like Pierre, his ghost appears younger than
he is. (But in fact he has turned forty.)
Beautifully-cut tweed suit. A bow-tie
which would seem to suggest a slight levity
of character. Good company, basically.
A ghost whose hand one would willingly
shake. Future uncertain.

DEUX FEMMES POUR UN FANTÔME was first performed on
22nd November 1971 at the *Théâtre de l'Oeuvre* in a production by
Pierre Franck. Décor by Jacques Noël.

TWO WOMEN FOR ONE GHOST

A Psychosomatic Comedy

Preface

Brigitte, the wife of Pierre, has only recently learned of her husband's affair with Viviane; she is distraught. She begs Viviane, whom she has never met before, to visit her while her husband is away on business, in order to 'clarify the situation'. Viviane responds.

What neither of the women knows is how pointless their discussion is. Pierre has in fact at that very moment been killed at the wheel of his car. The desire shared by both women to possess this man and reduce him to the different image each one has created in her mind no longer has any meaning. He has 'passed over'. And for a brief spell Pierre, who all at once finds himself 'on the other side', is going to haunt his own apartment and surprise his wife and mistress alone together. But they can neither see nor hear him. What does he care? Our 'fresh corpse' has preoccupations of a different kind. The psychological observations, often contradictory ones, proclaimed by the two women about his disposition, are far removed from the hidden reality of this man, the only reality by which he can justify his existence before an invisible Tribunal.

Considered in this light, the arguments of Brigitte and Viviane can but appear unreal and dolefully funny.

Production notes

In this play the producer will try and find a sort of 'ghost writing': to establish a constant awareness of the ghostly presence in relation to the two women so that the ghost adds a third dimension to the dialogue. He could, for example, at certain moments, find himself caught half-way between the two women, so that they seem to be talking right through him. Or sit down at the same time as one of the others, or be standing in the way just as Brigitte decides to go upstairs, or get passionately absorbed in some part of the conversation or deliberately move away to the other side of the room, etc.

His behaviour should always induce a feeling of something strange, even disquieting.

The ghost's movements will be buoyant and dance-like, as if the atmosphere of his world were liquid, giving at times a 'slow-motion' effect. He should in any case never touch the objects in the room. The only things he treats as material objects will be his hat, his folding-stool and his leather briefcase. When at the end he places the rose in the vase in front of his portrait, he will conjure it out of the air in a flash, like a magician.

Scene One

The action is set in BRIGITTE FREYCINET'S *official drawing-room.
Or, should one say, her husband* PIERRE'S? *A bourgeois drawing-
room, fairly luxurious but without much character, in spite of some
vague pretention at interior design.*
*Wood-panelling; hunting pictures; a tall mirror; an illuminated glass
cabinet containing knick-knacks; corner bookshelves gracefully
animated by a philodendron. If possible, a grand piano. (Grand, or
otherwise, it is worth noting that this instrument has practically
vanished from modern drawing-rooms.)*
A staircase leading from the room.
*In one corner, all the modern gear: a television set shielded by a
Chinese screen; record-player; hi-fi.*
*In the foreground, near a low table, a few chairs and a trolley
carrying numerous bottles of spirits. An ice-bucket; excellent carpets.*
When the curtain rises, BRIGITTE, *dressed in a sober tailored-suit, is
examining herself in front of the mirror, indulging in her feminine
rites. She is pale and drawn. Her eyes—she has failed to dispel the dark
circles—appear to be gazing at a stranger. However much she tries
pinching her lips, pulling at her cheeks or rubbing her nose with her
fingers, the blood refuses to rise to her face.*
*She has hardly slept for ten days, ever since she discovered (entirely
by chance) the affair between* PIERRE *and* VIVIANE. *For ten days
she has refused to believe it is really serious—it was just an accident!
Merely incidental! Men are weak, stupidly sensual, stupidly . . .
especially* PIERRE. *He's reached the age when . . . I must prove my
virility. A Don Juan every Sunday—no, every Friday. Ridiculous;
horribly familiar. But why* VIVIANE? *I'd have understood better if
it had been some twenty-year-old dolly. A dolly bird. For ten days
and ten nights she's been turning it over in her mind. She is worn to
a shadow of herself.*
Extremely nervous, BRIGITTE *never stops looking at her watch.*
A huge doll occupies one of the armchairs.

BRIGITTE (*marching up and down the room*).   Piano, piano,
    Brigitte, calm down. Sei ruhig, mein Kind, sei ruhig. Ma non
    troppo. Mollo. Piano. Don't get in such a state. She'll come all
    right, she's not late . . . and in Paris, you're never late, even if you
    are. Unless you've come on the wrong day . . . Calm down,
    Brigitte, calm down. Control yourself. Piano . . . Piano.

9

BRIGITTE *is constantly on the move from one end of the drawing-room to the other. She picks up a bottle of gin from the trolley and pours into a large glass an amount that one could hardly call negligible, but which is at least accompanied by a little water. After taking a drink:*

When she's come, she'll be here . . . She will be here! (*Miming the scene*) Come in, Madame, come in. This *is* the right place . . . You had no trouble finding it? . . . With all the one-way streets! . . . And all the roads up too! The Public Works: the extension of the Telephone Services, the Regional Underground Express, the Carolingian excavations . . . Come in, Miss, Madame, Mistress, my husband's Mistress Mine . . . (*She addresses the doll.*) Her Majesty the Queen of Tarts . . . I'm only his wife, his humble servant, his bowl of porridge . . . do take a seat, Madame, ascend upon this throne! I kiss the hem of your robe. The dust rises and falls as you pass, tracing out letters of gold. Your breath is like the honey tongue of the West Winds. Your ivory hands confound the rosy-fingered dawn . . . Oh, bugger! (*Without quite knowing why,* BRIGITTE *takes off her shoes and places them on the table.*) I could stand on my dignity. Get on my high horse. Drape myself in injured pride. (*She makes for the staircase, climbs a few steps and then, striking an inviolable pose, still addressing the doll.*) What precisely does Madame desire? (*Doing the questions and the answers*)
I desire your husband.
"Very original!"
And I may say he desires me too.
"Clifton's law."
I beg your pardon?
"Clifton's law, the law that governs magnetic attraction: when a magnetized body, adrift in space, meets another body in inverse proportion to the square of its distance . . . Forgive me, I am trying to 'unhackney' the situation."
because you find . . .
"It's so hackneyed, Madame, it makes me weep . . . " (*On the point of weeping.*)
You're not going to get weepy, Brigitte, are you? . . . You were saying, Madame?
"Pierre and I can't live without each other any more. We can't go on living without this . . . desire, without the genetic exaltation that possesses us. (*Stopping short and coldly*) 'Genetic exaltation that possesses us' I quote, it's in his letter. What a style! . . . Silly bitch! . . . (*Continuing lyrically*) Yes, as I was saying, without that genetic, biotic and apostolic exaltation, the days and the nights enshroud us in blankets of fur. Pierre and I feel as if we were plunging into a desert . . ."
A desert. And I myself, I am nothing but sand. A statue of sand. Blow,

dear lady, Sultana of Sultanas, blow hard and you'll blow me
away. (*She blows.*) There, I no longer exist . . . A handful of sand
running through your fingers . . . I no longer exist, I have never
existed. Until today I was only pretending. It was all just a joke.
It was just . . . while I was waiting for you . . . And while I'm
waiting, with your permission, I'll put on a little music: The
Piano Sonata by Brezhnev.

BRIGITTE *goes to the record-player and pulls out a record. We hear
the opening bars of the Third Piano Sonata by Brezhnev. A ring at
the front door.*

It is just as though BRIGITTE *had received an electric shock.*

*She stops the music, rushes to put on her shoes, swallows the rest
of the gin, inspects herself one last time in front of the mirror, hurls
the doll into the wings, and goes to open the door.*

Scene Two

VIVIANE (*off*). Madame Freycinet?
BRIGITTE (*off*). This *is* the right place. Come in. I was expecting
   you.

BRIGITTE *shows* VIVIANE *in.* VIVIANE *is wearing a leather raincoat,
very chic. She has made the most of herself. Perfect make-up and hair-
do. They are both wearing the same silk scarf. A moment of ill-
concealed surprise.* VIVIANE *takes off her scarf and slips it neatly
into her pocket. Both women are extremely self-conscious.*

BRIGITTE. You had no trouble finding it?
VIVIANE. I got lost once or twice . . . with all those one-way streets . . .
BRIGITTE (*extremely nervous and getting muddled*). One way or
   another. And all the roads up too! Works in progress: extensions
   of the telephone excavations, the Carolingian Underground, the
   Express . . . It's hard to put one foot in front of the other. And as
   for parking!
VIVIANE. I'm sorry I'm late.
BRIGITTE. But you're not late at all!
VIVIANE. Yes, I am a little late.
BRIGITTE. A little. I was expecting you, anyway. (*A slight pause.*)
VIVIANE. Still, I managed to park not too far away.
BRIGITTE. In the Rue Camembert, perhaps?
VIVIANE. Perhaps, I don't know.
BRIGITTE. You can still find a few spaces there. One can't help
   wondering why.
VIVIANE. Yes, one can't help wondering. (*A slight pause.*)
BRIGITTE. But do come in—we seem to have got stuck . . . and

don't mind the mess. No matter how much you tidy up, there's always something that escapes the eye at the last moment . . . All these newspapers, for example. (*She nervously gathers up a pile of newspapers from one armchair, only to put them down again on another almost next to it. A magazine has fallen to the floor.* VIVIANE *hurries to pick it up and holds it out to* BRIGITTE.) Thanks. They're just old newspapers and magazines, but Pierre likes to hang on to old things . . . He's very conservative—as you might say.

VIVIANE. As you might say.

BRIGITTE (*After tidying up the pile of newspapers*). There . . . come over here, we'll be more comfortable. (*She draws the visitor downstage.* VIVIANE *is in bright light.* BRIGITTE *contemplates her in silence for a while, and then, painfully)* So this is you!

VIVIANE (*Not knowing how to answer*). Yes, this is me.

BRIGITTE. As pretty as he said you were.

VIVIANE. Thanks. (BRIGITTE *hides her head in her hands as though afraid to take in the unbearable sight of her rival.*) . . . You're not going to start crying!

BRIGITTE (*composing herself*). Forgive me . . . seeing you in front of me 'in the flesh' . . . yes, really very pretty. Your eyes, your mouth, the curve of your eyebrows . . . Pierre told me about the curve of your eyebrows.

VIVIANE. Oh yes? (*With a deliberately light touch*) Nowadays, you know, a woman can invent all her curves.

BRIGITTE (*continuing to anatomise her*). Your nose, the way you tilt your head when you say something, the way you hold yourself . . .

VIVIANE. I tilt my head when I talk!

BRIGITTE. It's always through other people's eyes that we're seen . . . the slope of your shoulders, your ankles and wrists—such fine bones you have, Pierre didn't mislead me.

VIVIANE (*forcing herself to take it lightly*). Well! I hope he also told you about . . .

BRIGITTE. . . . About your breasts, your thighs and your waist . . .

VIVIANE (*as though mortified*). I'd never have thought that Petrov . . .

BRIGITTE. Petrov! You call him Petrov!

VIVIANE. You call him Pierre, I suppose.

BRIGITTE. Pierre is his name and his name has always been Pierre . . . Petrov!! What a laugh! (*A horribly nervous little laugh.*)

VIVIANE. Laugh if you like!

BRIGITTE. Oh! I'm not laughing. There's really nothing to laugh about.

VIVIANE (*drily*). No, really there isn't.

BRIGITTE. But when I think . . . (*She laughs.*) Forgive me, it's just nerves. That Russian name all of a sudden—and he's such a reactionary, so Atlantic Pact . . . (*She cries.*)

VIVIANE. Atlantic Pact! (BRIGITTE *is shaken by sobs.* VIVIANE *feels very uncomfortable.*) . . . Please now, Brigitte, (*Correcting herself*) Madame.

BRIGITTE (*Sorrowfully*).   Oh! You might as well call me Brigitte.

IVIANE.   He's talked so much about you . . .

BRIGITTE (*Her poor little face lighting up*). Really? Does he often talk about me?

IVIANE.   I mean . . . when we've the time.

RIGITTE.   . . . Of course. That's . . . that's only human. (*She starts crying again.*)

IVIANE.   I should never have come!

RIGITTE.   But I'm glad you did! I'm really very grateful to you. Answering my appeal so quickly.

IVIANE.   I like clear-cut situations.

RIGITTE.   So you kidnap my husband twice a week!

IVIANE (*Volubly*).   You didn't know. And I knew you didn't know. Petrov, (*correcting herself*) Pierre knew very well that, if I'd known that you knew, I'd rather have let you know at once, even before there was anything between us. Then there would never have been anything, of course, so in fact I wouldn't have had anything to tell you. And that's why I never said anything . . . Don't take any notice, I express myself badly. I feel pretty emotional too. (BRIGITTE *has moved up to the trolley, followed by* VIVIANE. *She pours herself a drink.*)

RIGITTE.   I'm having gin. For ten days now it's been gin. (*Preparing to serve* VIVIANE) But perhaps you prefer whisky. Or Carpano?

IVIANE.   Yes, whisky.

RIGITTE.   With water? Flat or volcanic?

IVIANE.   Volcanic! That's the same expression as Pet . . . By itself. No water. No, no ice, thanks.

RIGITTE.   Straight.

IVIANE.   Straight.

RIGITTE (*pouring out her whisky*). I'm sorry. I just realised I served myself first.

IVIANE.   You ought to come first . . . I mean . . . No, no. Not too much. Not too much. You don't mind? (*She pours the excess whisky back into the bottle.*) . . . There. Perfect.

RIGITTE.   You want to keep your head!

IVIANE.   No, I've lost it more than once, you know. You mustn't think I . . .

RIGITTE.   I mustn't think you . . . ?

IVIANE.   Nothing, nothing . . . It's too difficult just now.

RIGITTE (*raising her glass*). Well then . . . we drink to . . . we drink to Petrov! (*Without even putting her lips to the glass, she sets it down again and sobs.*)

IVIANE (*in consternation*). Madame! . . . Brigitte . . . Madame Brigitte! . . . It was wrong of me to come, I see that now. If you like, we can put our talk off till later, when you feel more relaxed.

BRIGITTE. I've lost all my old self-control. Since I first heard of you
affair with Pierre ten days ago, I've not been able to sleep, I can't
eat and I've not been out . . . I drink, I smoke, I pace up and down
like a caged animal. And I've hardly the strength left for that. A
limp rag. You see what I am: a limp rag . . . And yet I promised
myself I would . . .

VIVIANE (*Almost an outburst*). But after all, you must have
suspected something?

BRIGITTE. I don't know. I don't know any more . . . yes, yes, yes.
Yes and no . . . Obviously, I should have been on my guard.
Pierre was being nicer and nicer to me. You know what men are?

VIVIANE. We know.

BRIGITTE. If every time he . . . I'd had to . . .

VIVIANE. Every time he . . . ?

BRIGITTE. Nothing, nothing. It's too difficult just now.

VIVIANE (*passing her the glass of gin*). Here, drink! Let's drink!
(*With forced joviality*) We're going to get high, gain altitude,
the two of us. (*They both drink.*)

BRIGITTE. It's terrible. I like you. I really like you.

VIVIANE. I know how you feel, it's the same . . .

BRIGITTE. I hate you, yet I don't seem able to hate you . . . Viviane
that *is* your name?

VIVIANE. Viviane.

BRIGITTE. And . . . he calls you Viviane?

VIVIANE. Yes, he calls me Viviane.

BRIGITTE (*more to herself*). Viviane! It's much prettier than Brigitte
more erotic . . . two opening arms, or thighs . . .

VIVIANE. Well, I . . . !!

BRIGITTE. Because of the two V's, I suppose. Viviane. (*Maliciously*)
For ten days I've been saying your name, over and over again from
morning till night. Viviane, Viviana, Lana the Liana, Viviana the
Sultana, Sultanissima, Vivvy the skivvy, vivacious Viv the
vivisectionist! Viviane! Viviane! . . . For ten days without a stop I've
been playing a hate game with your name. Hate! Yes, night and
day, I've been hating you. (*She sobs.*)

VIVIANE. We've no chance of communicating, if things go on like th
Please try and keep calm, Madame!

BRIGITTE (*rectifying*). Brigitte.

VIVIANE. Brigitte, don't cry! Follow my example. Do you think I'm
iceberg?

BRIGITTE (*vehemently*). Oh no! Definitely not! Oh no!

VIVIANE. From the moment I knew that you knew, and that Petr . .
that Pierre . . . I can't sleep either, I can't eat, I go to the office, and
back home again, as if I'm walking in my sleep . . . And Pierre, tell m
how is he at the moment? I haven't seen him since, not for nearly a
week . . . not since . . .

BRIGITTE. I know.

VIVIANE. What sort of state . . .?

BRIGITTE. He can't sleep. He can't eat. He watches the telly.

VIVIANE. It's absurd. It's all quite absurd. (*A pause.*) . . . It may
seem odd to you, but when you phoned me yesterday I was
relieved—yes, relieved. (*The sound of a fire engine.* BRIGITTE *is
unable to check her flood of tears.*). . . . On my way here I saw
myself chatting to you, reasonably. So far as one can ever be
reasonable where love is concerned. (*The fire engine again, closer
this time.*)

BRIGITTE (*through her tears*). Even the firemen are joining in!

VIVIANE. Yes, reasonably. We're not kids any more. We should be
able to discuss things together, if not as friends, at least like two
sisters—two grown-up sisters still sharing the same bed . . . Damn, I
really do express myself badly. (*She resolutely pours herself a
tumblerful of whisky.*)

BRIGITTE (*horribly startled by the* 'same bed'). The same bed! I
hope you've never been here before?

VIVIANE (*A brazen but charitable lie*). Never. I swear I haven't!

BRIGITTE. It would hurt me terribly to think . . . And Pierre
knows nothing at all about our meeting? You promised me that.

VIVIANE. I never said a word.

BRIGITTE (*bewildered*). Where is he, anyway, at the moment?

VIVIAN. In Orléans.

BRIGITTE. Ah yes! It's his day for Orléans.

VIVIANE. It's today he's got to make his speech.

BRIGITTE. That's right. I ought to know it by heart by now,
after the time he's spent practising in front of the mirror: we
welcome here tonight the Minister of this, the President of that,
General So-and-so, Honourable Members . . . (*They drink. Heavy
embarrassed silence.*)

VIVIANE (*for something to say, timidly*). You know Orléans?

BRIGITTE. Not really . . . I've never lived there.

VIVIANE. It's full of streets and shops and cinemas, swimming
pools, petrol pumps, and drugstores . . . (*Pause.*) It's pretty dead
at night. But there *is* the Loire.

BRIGITTE (*blankly*). The famous river.

VIVIANE. And then, of course, those souvenirs of Joan of Arc.

BRIGITTE. And God knows what else! (*Loud noise of a fire engine.*)

VIVIANE. Must be a blazing furnace, to judge by the fire engines
racing by . . . (*Pause.*) There aren't nearly so many fires here as there
are in New York, luckily. (*Pause.*) You know New York?

BRIGITTE. Pierre does, yes. But not me.

VIVIANE. In New York, if it's not one house, it's another . . .
especially in the poorer districts. All made of wood. (*Silence.*) What
with that and all their electric gadgets. You go off to work in the
morning and put the leg of mutton in the supersonic oven set for

7.22 . . . And at 7.22 precisely, boned and ready to eat, it pops straight into your mouth. But if there's a hint of a short circuit while you're out! . . . Not to mention their ash-cans! Tons of rotting rubbish all over the sidewalks, right into the middle of the street—such a filthy mess! Cardboard boxes, newspapers, mangy old bits of fur . . .

BRIGITTE. There must be lots of rats?

VIVIANE (*surprised*). Rats? I never saw any rats. You're right, logically there ought to be lots of rats . . . but I came across lots of dogs. The number of dogs there are, trotting around in New York! All dressed up. Permed and lacquered. But all those dogs, I suppose it's because of the mugging . . . even a little dog barks . . . And then, one mustn't forget the homosexuals.

BRIGITTE (*Suddenly taking her by the hand*). Go on, please go on! Say whatever comes into your head, however silly it is . . . It'll make me feel better. I'm beginning to get used to you . . . I've simply got to try very hard to stop undressing you . . . (*Sharp reaction from* VIVIANE.) . . . I can't help seeing you stark naked. Even with my eyes shut, you're stark naked . . . And just look! You've still got your coat on. Why don' you take it off!

VIVIANE (*Extremely disturbed*). My coat! Why, yes! So I have.

When VIVIANE *removes her coat, she could be wearing a dress that is vis the same as* BRIGITTE's. *The same pattern, for example, but with the colot reversed. Another source of comic embarrassment between the two wome*

BRIGITTE. Throw it down anywhere.

VIVIENNE (*Throwing it on the back of a chair*). There. (*She smooths her skirt out with a determined gesture, buttons up her blouse, which is generously revealing.*)

BRIGITTE (*Pouring herself a drink*). Gin for me. (*Glancing rapidly in the mirror.*) God, how ugly I look! It's terrible how ugly I've become in th last ten days! . . . All that stupid crying . . . If you don't mind I'll go to the bathroom and do something about my make-up. I'm ashamed to let you see me like this. (*She drinks. Going out to the bathroom*) Just give me two minutes.

VIVIANE. Please go ahead. (*Left on her own, she pours herself a drink. Standing up, with her glass in her hand, she strolls round the room. She inspects it without any particular interest: she has already been in* PIERRE's *apartment several times, while* BRIGITTE *was away. As she walks about*) . . . I know it all by heart. *I* didn't want to. But Petro insisted.

She sits down, opens a magazine, then closes it almost at once: her mind is elsewhere. She is living through the moment when she first came into her lover's apartment.

The sound of a key in the door. The door opens.

PIERRE (*Off, happily*). Into the wolf's lair, little lamb!

IVIANE (*laughing*). Baaaaa . . .

IERRE (*Off, laughing*). You're impossible! . . . The switch on
the left, just there on the left . . . Bravo! . . . Your coat. Why
don't you like it off. (*Short pause.*) Throw it down anywhere.

IVIANE. I never imagined your flat would look like this!

IERRE (*Off, slightly upset*). How *did* you imagine it!?

IVIANE. I don't know . . . not so bourgeois.

IERRE (*Off*). It's because of Brigitte. She's fond of her
family furniture. I'd have chucked out all this junk long ago
. . . (*A fairly long pause. In velvet tones*) Take your clothes
off!

IVIANE. Straight away?

IERRE (*Off, cheerfully growing more idiotic*). Straight away, my
proud beauty, at once. Expresso. Mikado. Coco. Cocoyannis.
Prestissimo. Motel me that you love me.

IVIANE. You fool! (*A pause; then in an extremely ambiguous
tone of voice*) Petrov! Petrov! . . . Petrov, what are you playing
at? . . . Petrov!

IERRE (*Off, greedily*). Peeping Tom. The vigilant vicar. The
villainous voyeur! Don't look now, but . . . (*A pause.*) . . . And now
you walk up the staircase and come down again, just as you are
right now . . .

IVIANE. Petrov! We are *not* at the Casino de Paris!

IERRE (*Off, holding back his simmering emotion*). A naked woman
walking up and down a staircase, you can't imagine how that
excites me!

The screaming siren of a fire engine. The effect of this is to bring
IVIANE back to the reality of the moment.

IVIANE (*going to the window*). What, again! (*She comes back
and sits down again. She picks up a photograph of* PIERRE.
A pause.)

PIERRE (*Off*). Shall I put a record on? . . . Chopin, Brahms, Buxtehude?

IVIANE. I hate Brahms.

PIERRE (*Off*). Jo Bingwell. You like Jo Bingwell? 'No Man's Land'.

IVIANE. Not now, Petrov. All these modern records that go on
and on . . . (*A slight pause. Then, suddenly, anxiously*) You're sure
Brigitte won't come back?

BRIGITTE (*coming back from the bathroom*). Here I am! (VIVIANE
has sprung out of her seat, as though caught in the act. BRIGITTE
*has made herself up and done her hair. She is trying to put a
new face on things.*) I'm sorry about just now. I promise I'll be
more sensible . . . Won't you have another drink?

VIVIANE. Yes. A little. (*She holds out her glass.* BRIGITTE
pours herself one too. They both drink.)

BRIGITTE (*putting down her glass*). Right against doctor's
orders, with the pills I've been taking.

VIVIANE.   You shouldn't, then.
BRIGITTE.   What the hell . . . (*A slight pause. Then, asking her ques*
   quietly, not at all aggressive) . . . Have you been with him
   before, to Orléans?
VIVIANE.   Yes.
BRIGITTE.   You went regularly?
VIVIANE.   Regularly.
BRIGITTE.   On Fridays?
VIVIANE.   Yes, on Fridays. (*A Pause.*)
BRIGITTE (*mildly perfidious*).   And Poitiers?
VIVIANE (*as though bitten by a viper*).   How do you mean, Poitiers?
BRIGITTE.   On the days he goes to Poitiers. That's not you?
VIVIANE (*exploding*).   That's a lie! There are no days for Poitiers.
   Or for Bordeaux, or Clermont-Ferrand. If you're trying to . . .
   you're lying!
BRIGITTE.   Don't get worked up! There is no day for Poitiers . . .
   How you must love him!
VIVIANE (*trying to control herself*).   Brigitte, listen. We are both abl
   to hurt each other. Let's try to . . .
BRIGITTE.   I'm trying to hurt you?! I didn't know you even existed.
   You were born ten days ago. You're a fine one to say that! You're
   the one who has broken up our home. You're the one who . . .
VIVIANE (*getting carried away*).   I never broke anything up, I'm sorr
   to say! I mean, I refuse to say that. I can even quote you a remark
   of Pierre's . . . (*She hesitates*) 'If I stay with Brigitte, it's thanks to
   you.'
BRIGITTE (*coldly*).   That's a classic.
VIVIANE.   What on earth do you mean?
BRIGITTE.   A classic. Chopin, Brahms, Buxtehude, and all that jazz.
   I detest Brahms. Shall I put a record on?
VIVIANE.   For God's sake, Brigitte . . .
BRIGITTE.   A classic. Thanks to your good offices, Pierre does me a
   favour. (*She drinks.*) Perhaps I should invite you to move in, so you
   can keep a better eye on our domestic scene? . . . What are you doi
   (VIVIANE *has risen to her feet. She has picked up her coat.*)
VIVIANE.   I'm going.
BRIGITTE (*humbly entreating*).   Please, please don't go. Forgive me .
   I love Pierre. I never quite realized until today how much I loved
   him.
VIVIANE.   A classic! (*Very quietly*) What exactly did Pierre tell you
   about our affair?
BRIGITTE (*sadly*).   The truth.
VIVIANE (*almost teasing*).   The truth?!
BRIGITTE.   Yes, I'm sure it was. Once Pierre stops lying, he's always
   brutally frank. (*Pause.*) It's nearly a year ago that you met. You're
   divorced and you're bringing up your little boy on your own.
   Alexandre.

VIVIANE.   Alexandre. It's funny to hear you saying his name!

BRIGITTE (*in the style of a fortune-teller, with a blank stare, mechanically*).   You have courage, a happy disposition, and the agency where you work thinks highly of you. You speak several languages fluently. You enjoy driving at night. Rowing and riding. You hate games. You suffer from tachycardia. You're mad about shellfish.

VIVIANE (*dumbfounded by the truthfulness of* BRIGITTE'S *reading*).   My God!

BRIGITTE (*more and more mechanically*).   Difficult childhood. Your mother and father didn't get on. You suffered a lot from that. That's why you married very young. Too young . . . Your husband had plenty of good will, but unfortunately no will-power. Completely dominated by his sister, Louise. She hated you. You could hardly have known, before you married your husband Georges, that you'd be marrying Louise, his sister, too. You put up with a lot of things till Alexandre was born. But you couldn't stand the idea that your son, Alexandre, should also become the son of your sister-in-law, Louise, the sister of Georges, your husband, the father of Alexandre.

VIVIANE.   Go on! Go on!

BRIGITTE (*all of a sudden, quite natural*).   You'd have loved to take up painting. (*A slight pause.*) Poor Pierre.

VIVIANE (*annoyed*).   Why poor Pierre?

BRIGITTE.   Because you dragged him round all the exhibitions, and there's nothing he finds more exasperating than having to tramp round galleries and museums—those concentration camps as he calls them.

VIVIANE.   The Pierre who comes with me to exhibitions may not be quite the same Pierre as the man you waltz off to strip-tease clubs . . .

BRIGITTE.   Ah! You've heard about that.

VIVIANE.   We know all about each other. Anyone would think that Pierre was using us as communicating vessels, to try out some scientific theory. (*Picking up* BRIGITTE's *former tone of voice*) . . . You enjoy receptions, theatre, ballet, anything that has a certain glamour: travelling abroad—providing the hotels are quite luxurious. You're sensitive about conventions, about style. You chase after antiques. You're clever with your hands—interior decoration appealed to you for a time—you loathe the organ.

BRIGITTE.   Go on! go on!

VIVIANE (*very liberated*).   You're highly-sexed and clitoris-fixated.

BRIGITTE (*speechless*).   Viviane!

VIVIANE.   Perhaps we should call a halt at this point?

BRIGITTE.   Yes, I think it would be best . . . in any case, it's not
getting us anywhere. A little more whisky?

VIVIANE *holds out her glass.* BRIGITTE *pours her out some
whisky and serves herself a gin. The two women drink in silence.
This is the moment when* PIERRE *makes his appearance.*

PIERRE *or more precisely* PIERRE's *ghost comes straight through
the wall. Light overcoat, little soft trilby hat, a leather briefcase under
one arm and holding a folding-stool.* BRIGITTE *and* VIVIANE *do
not see him and will not see him throughout the next scene.*

*Every time the phantom speaks, the gestures made by the two
women will be in slow motion, so that they give a dream-like
impression.*
In addition, every time PIERRE's *ghost comes near* BRIGITTE, *she
feels icy cold. Every time he is beside* VIVIANE, *she, on the other
hand, feels waves of heat.*

Scene Three

GHOST (*He has come forward to the edge of the stage. In a voice
that is astonished and almost joyful*).
I am dead.
I am dead.
I died a few seconds ago, at the wheel of the car.
Fly away, motor!
Fly away, wheels!
Windows in pieces!
The brain just reels!

A new car.
Yes, my wife pushed me into buying a new car. (*Imitating her*) 'you
an executive! In an old bus that dates from the Hundred Years War!
Do you want to make the grade or don't you?'
A new car. A Mercedes, SJ 3588 RQ. The road to Orléans.
A bend. A tree.
A lovely lovely tree.
Crash! Bang! Wallop!
End of me!
So good-day all!

*He sets his folding-stool up beside him, takes a thermos flask from his
briefcase and puts it down next to the folding-stool, lays his briefcase on
the stool and mops his brow with a large check handkerchief.*

BRIGITTE (*raising her glass*).   Skol!
VIVIANE (*raising her glass*).   Skol!

GHOST.   Talk about impact!
   No steering-wheel, no halo.
   Naked as a worm.
   A little sky-worm . . .

   And now here are my two women at one fell swoop!
   At one fell swoop!
   Busy knocking back my spirits!

*In an attempt to attract their attention, he whistles. The two women
exchange a sort of smile.*

   It's not important.
   Anyway, they can't see me.
   They can't hear me.
   They can neither see nor hear me.
   Thousands of stars between us.
   Thousands of words fragmented into stars.
   Nebulas . . .
VIVIANE (*as a shiver runs over her, after taking a drink*). Your
   whisky would galvanise a corpse!
BRIGITTE.   I beg your pardon?
VIVIANE.   I said your whisky packs a punch!
BRIGITTE.   It's very good, but not old enough yet.
VIVIANE.   One has to admit that nowadays there's less and less
   time to grow old.
BRIGITTE.   That's true . . . the way History races on . . .
GHOST.   What are they talking about? And what are they doing, the
   two of them together anyway? (*Shouting out*) What's all this farcical
   nonsense? . . . One was called Viviane, and the other's name was
   . . . was . . . (*He searches through his feeble memory.*) Brigitte!
   No . . . no, the other one was called Viviane.
BRIGITTE.   Viviane?
VIVIANE.   Yes?
BRIGITTE.   You don't mind if I call you Viviane?
VIVIANE.   Viviane, Vivvy, vivacious Viv the vivisectionist . . .
BRIGITTE.   It's all quite different now you're here. (*A sudden fit of
   shivering*) Brrrr! It's so cold all of a sudden. Don't you feel the cold?
VIVIANE.   I'm stifling. (*She undoes a button at her neck.*)
BRIGITTE.   Yet the windows are closed!
VIVIANE.   It's all the pills you're taking.
GHOST (*mopping his brow*).   Streaming, too!
   Soaking wet.
   Yet I'm not sweating.
   Strange.
   (*Pause.*)
   This is quite a day!

BRIGITTE.   Viviane, if I asked you to come here, it's above all
because I'd like to try and grasp it, to understand . . . if Pierre
had lost his head for a young thing of twenty, one of those
nymphets you see all around these days, in dungarees . . .

GHOST.   No Man's Land.
I must be in No Man's Land . . .
(*He takes the cork out of his thermos flask.*)

BRIGITTE.   . . . What has Pierre got against me? What is there that I
can't give him and you can? . . . What does he tell *you,* when he
talks about me?

VIVIANE.   He says he married a quite exceptional woman. That
you're faithful, straightforward, generous . . .

BRIGITTE.   Healthy, stable and sober! What is it then? What?
(*Beside herself*) It's all a matter of skin? (*Shouting*) A matter of
skin!

GHOST.   Crash, bang, wallop! Right through the shell.
Like the sun bursting out of an egg.
With the blood seeping out.
The blood.
Sunflower, convolvulus, poppy, a poppy-like sun.
A hard-boiled sun.
(*Singing to the two women.*)
Oh don't deceive me,
Oh never leave me,
How could you use a poor phantom so . . .

BRIGITTE.   I'm sorry to say I read your letters.

VIVIANE (*Sharp reaction*).   Pierre swore to me he'd burn all my
letters!

BRIGITTE.   It was just like re-reading the ones I sent him, before
we were married.

VIVIANE (*extremely put out*).   One love letter is depressingly like
another.

BRIGITTE.   Apart from the fact that you're far more indecent that I
am. You're not afraid of words. I could quote you some passages
by heart. (*Reciting*) 'My beloved Russian Prince' (*Suddenly seeing
the point*) Oh! now I've got it: Petrov!

GHOST (*with a great welcoming gesture to* VIVIANE).   Petrov!

BRIGITTE.   And I was stupidly wondering why all that Russification.

VIVIANE.   Pierre mentioned your tact too!

BRIGITTE (*woefully*).   I'm sorry, that was deplorable . . . (*Slight
pause.*) Pierre, if I understand you, finds my good qualities too
much for him.

VIVIANE.   No, no, it's not that. It's not so simple.

BRIGITTE.   With Pierre it was simple for years and years,
marvellously simple.

VIVIANE (*gently*).   It would appear that it wasn't quite like that . . .

BRIGITTE. Then how do you explain . . .

VIVIANE. I can't explain anything. I confess that, when you found
out about us, I was surprised by Pierre's attitude: utter collapse.
Tranquillising pills and drops. Ice bags clapped to his head . . .
end of Pierre.

GHOST. Crash, bang, wallop! End of me.
A hard-boiled sun.
A bed of crimson clouds.
And that triangular eye.
That eye!

BRIGITTE. He was always absurdly over-sensitive.

VIVIANE. Emotional.

BRIGITTE. Very emotional

GHOST. A bearded man.
A blue bearded man.
Bluebearded.
A big bearded man.
Quite blue.
With fire in his beard.
Fire! Fire!
(*Fire siren.*)

BRIGITTE (*startled by the siren*). What, again! It's an absolute
mania! . . . I'm sorry.

VIVIANE. But it's not your fault.

BRIGITTE. No, I suppose it isn't. (*A pause.*)

VIVIANE. You see . . . just to try to answer your question . . .
every man . . . (*She hesitates before going on.*) . . . every man—and
Pierre in particular—has something shadowy about him, a dark
core of hidden depths . . . Perhaps, without realising it, even
because you're so attached to him, you denied him that invisible
part of himself.

GHOST. Let me get my breath back.
That very last breath.
(*He breathes in noisily.*)

BRIGITTE (*maliciously*). And what's this ghost of himself really
like? Do you know the right diet to give him? Is he good company?
Is he good in bed?

VIVIANE. You promised you'd be reasonable.

BRIGITTE. It's hard not to be jealous . . . (*She pours herself some
gin.*)

GHOST. A little coffee.
(*He opens the thermos flask, pours the liquid into the cup and
drinks with a satisfied air.*)

VIVIANE. Don't drink, you'll only make yourself worse.

BRIGITTE. When I've downed a certain number of glasses, I get
very cheerful. I even end up laughing at my own misfortunes.

VIVIANE. Pierre is always saying: Life is a tragedy for those who
feel . . .

BRIGITTE & VIVIANE (*together*). . . . and a comedy for those
who think.

BRIGITTE.   He's been trotting that out for twelve years. And he
must have given you the privilege of hearing this one too: 'Everyone
is as God made him . . . (*Together*) . . . and very often worse!'

They both laugh.
The GHOST's *face glows with a look of genuine satisfaction at*
hearing himself quoted. While the two women were saying the last
words, he was mouthing them silently at the same time.

BRIGITTE.   Pierre always has one of these striking phrases held in
reserve. They make him appear to others more intelligent than
he really is.

VIVIANE (*quickly*).   You're not going to refuse Pierre his intelligence!

BRIGITTE.   I never said Pierre wasn't intelligent!

A pause. VIVIANE, *who is beginning to fall quite seriously under the*
influence of the whisky, places her hand on BRIGITTE's.

VIVIANE.   It's awful: you know I find you're quite nice too.

BRIGITTE.   Thanks.

VIVIANE.   I imagined you quite different.

BRIGITTE.   Expecting to meet a dragon?

VIVIANE.   No, not that, of course. Petrov . . . Pierre always talked of
you in a very . . . positive way. But, I don't know why, I imagined
you rather cold, rather sophisticated . . . not nearly so feminine.
(*With emphasis*) You're *very* feminine!

BRIGITTE (*shivering*).   Brrrr! . . . (*Turning towards* GHOST) Can't
you feel that freezing air?

VIVIANE.   I'm getting hotter and hotter.

BRIGITTE.   Brrrr! (*She suddenly stands up.*) Would you like me to
show you round the flat?

VIVIANE (*speechless*).   Would I . . .

BRIGITTE.   This is your lover's home. If I were in your shoes, I'd
be curious to . . . Just look, for example, this staircase . . .

VIVIANE.   What about the staircase?

BRIGITTE.   Well, that is Pierre's pride and joy.

VIVIANE.   Oh really?

BRIGITTE.   Pierre can't survive without an intimate private staircase.
It's because of the staircase that he chose this flat.

VIVIANE.   Oh really?

BRIGITTE.   Come along, and I'll let you see upstairs . . .

VIVIANE.   No, Brigitte, please. Stay here. Anyway, it's as if I knew it
all by heart.

GHOST.   You bet!

BRIGITTE (*sitting down again*).   Bourgeois, all much too bourgeois for
my taste.

VIVIANE. I wouldn't say that.

BRIGITTE. Oh yes, it is. A total lack of imagination. It's because
of Pierre. He's fond of his family furniture. I'd have chucked out
all this junk long ago . . . It's his conservative side. He's such a
reactionary.

VIVIANE. That's the second time you've told me Pierre is a reactionary.
Just now you even used a funny expression . . . (*She tries to
remember.*) Atlantic Pact!

GHOST (*in a sudden panic*). My speech! Did I bring my speech with
me? (*He opens his briefcase and feverishly takes out a large number
of files.*)

BRIGITTE. Yes, Atlantic Pact. Pierre is in favour. All for N.A.T.O.
(*Pompously*) To defend the sacred values of the western world.
An eternal subject of argument between us.

VIVIANE. You amaze me. Pierre is such an adventurer—in spirit,
I mean . . . He's so open-minded, so ready to vary his approach
. . . like most left-wingers.

BRIGITTE. Pierre, a left-winger! (*She laughs nervously.*) Perhaps
that depends on how you tell your left from your right.

GHOST (*trying to sort out his papers*). The Poirel file. The Bidard
file. The Mahut file . . . Not a sign of the speech . . . That would be
the end! (*He mops his brow.*)

VIVIANE. I mean that by nature he's for everything that's
progressive. Anything that changes, anything that's opposed to
those elements that alienate us. Why, only recently he was
applauding staggered strikes!

GHOST. They ought to stagger a lot more. Round and round,
like horses on a merry-go-round! Gallop into the backsides of the
dirty bourgeois beasts! (*The GHOST's intervention in the
dialogue between the two women is quite natural, but he never
speaks lines directly to them.*)

BRIGITTE. You stagger me!

VIVIANE. He used to talk too of establishing 'a state of permanent
terror'.

BRIGITTE. You stagger me. I'm quite staggered. During those recent
strikes, I mean, here in this very house, he did nothing but stomp up
and down in a raging fury and kick out at all the armchairs.

GHOST (*standing up and doing just that*). Yesterday, the Post Office.
Today the Railways. Tomorrow the Gas Company, the Electricity
Board, the Public Sector, the Private Sector. The day after tomorrow,
it'll be every bloody sector. No more hygiene, no more morality . . .
We ought to shoot a few of them, so they can taste the delights
of the Strike Eternal!

VIVIANE. You stupefy me. I am stupefied.

BRIGITTE. It's funny, when you come to think about it.

VIVIANE. You think it's funny?

BRIGITTE. Perhaps a man is a right-winger with his lawful spouse, and a left-winger with his mistress . . .

VIVIANE.   There's no sense in what you're saying. (*Suddenly feeling kind of dizzy*) Pooh! Those waves of heat that suddenly hit you! (*The* GHOST *is right beside her.*)

BRIGITTE.   Of heat?

VIVIANE.   Yes, I don't know what's the matter with me . . . it's as if from time to time an oven door was opened right beside me . . . Take no notice, it's my nerves.

BRIGITTE.   Right or left Pierre has the best of the bargain anyway!

VIVIANE.   Don't you believe it. Pierre detests duplicity. Our situation upset him terribly.

BRIGITTE.   If on top of all that he saw himself as unhappy!

VIVIANE.   Many, many's the time, just as he was leaving my place, when we'd had such a happy evening, he'd make some gloomy . . . (*Realising her blunder*) Oh! I'm sorry!

GHOST.   Right, now that's enough of this nonsense! On stage for the second act. I'm going to give Brigitte her cue. (*Sarcastically*) A faithful wife: and all she can do is get at me.

VIVIANE (*lovingly reproving him*).   Petrov!

GHOST.   Playing my part again, what fun!

BRIGITTE.   Admirably too. As if he'd been rehearsing all his life. From the cradle onwards

GHOST.   Oh! My little pigeon, those Board Meetings! They're an obsession! . . . Nowadays, it's not a matter of work, but of talking about work. Organising work. And organising the organisation. Bla, bla, bla . . .

BRIGITTE.   And did you speak too, darling?

GHOST.   Two hours without a stop, my little dove, two hours without a stop. Without notes. I'm exhausted, drained . . . I wouldn't mind a little tea.

VIVIANE.   Poor Petrov!

BRIGITTE.   I mean to say!

VIVIANE.   What do you expect? You've got to take life as it comes . . . We don't know what lies in wait when it's over . . . Will you give me a little more whisky? (BRIGITTE *pours one for* VIVIANE *and takes another gin herself. It will soon become apparent that* VIVIANE, *already 'under the influence', does not carry her liquor nearly as well as* BRIGITTE. VIVIANE *gulps it in one and puts down her glass.*) . . . Between ourselves, just between the two of us . . .

GHOST (*interrupting his search for a second*).
     That eye.
     That triangular eye.

BRIGITTE (*more than attentive*).   I'm listening.

VIVIANE.   But just think, if Pierre knew I was here . . .

BRIGITTE (*Her composure now contrasts with* VIVIANE's *tipsy state*). He won't know, I promise you. He'll never know. After all, we have a right to our little secrets too . . .

VIVIANE (*lyrically*).   If all the women in the world wanted to get
   it off their breasts . . .
BRIGITTE.   You wanted to tell me something?
GHOST.   Superb, that speech. Superb!
   (*Making an enormous effort of memory and addressing himself
   to the audience*)
   We welcome here tonight the Honourable Minister
   The Honorary President
   Right Reverend Sir
   Mr This
   Mr That
   Our Equatorial Commissioner . . . and then? . . . What comes
   next? . . .
   (*Irritated, to the two women*) Go on then! What's the cue?
BRIGITTE.   What was it you wanted to tell me?
VIVIANE.   Ah yes! (*She suddenly bursts out laughing.*) The fact
   that Petr . . . that Pierre had to play a part often led to comical
   situations.
BRIGITTE.   I don't doubt it!
VIVIANE.   For example—just one in a thousand—one evening . . .
BRIGITTE.   One of those Board Meeting evenings.
VIVIANE.   . . . when there was a Board Meeting, I'd prepared a
   delicious little supper for him, by candlelight.
BRIGITTE.   As in King Louis' golden days!

From now on, forgetting that BRIGITTE *is the victim,* VIVIANE
*chats away to her as though she were a very old friend, her confidant.
The* GHOST *sits down on his stool between the two women and
listens attentively.*

VIVIANE.   Caviar, foie gras, larks on toast, the Chef's cheese board,
   chocolate soufflé . . .
BRIGITTE.   Pierre loathes chocolate.
VIVIANE.   Not when it rises! Turkish coffee. Russian champagne . . .
BRIGITTE.   The whole works!
VIVIANE.   Well, the poor man . . .
BRIGITTE.   I like that!
VIVIANE.   . . . That evening, so as not to make you suspicious, he
   had already had an evening meal with you. You had boiled up
   some mutton stew.
BRIGITTE.   Pierre would go down on his knees for mutton stew.
VIVIANE.   So when I sat him down at my groaning table, you can
   just imagine! It was only when he'd struggled through to the end
   that he admitted he'd already had supper with you. He didn't
   want to hurt my feelings.
BRIGITTE.   A tact that does him credit.
VIVIANE (*living the scene through again*).   You should have seen
   him, picking and nibbling away at it! Three little caviar eggs, a

small crescent of foie gras, one minute lark's bone, a sliver of Roquefort, and a tiny dribble of champage to finish off . . . And the look on his face! Suddenly just like a muttonhead. It was as if that stew was seeping out of his ears, and his nostrils and his eyes! . . . How we laughed afterwards! (*She laughs*).

BRIGITTE (*sadly*).   Hilarious. Positively hilarious.

VIVIANE (*well away now*).   It's the same thing with films. The number of times he finds he's seen the film before!

BRIGITTE.   Am I to gather that you like the same films I do?

VIVIANE.   That's just it. Pierre's misfortune is that we two have the same tastes. You know, I have often wondered why, when a man takes a new woman, he always takes one exactly like the first? In a different form, of course.

BRIGITTE (*ironically*).   Now you've raised a question that deserves a sociological enquiry.

VIVIANE.   No, no. It's all so commonplace what I'm saying . . . And after all what's the point of talking about 'men' and 'women'? . . . It's just one man and one woman.

BRIGITTE.   You amuse me. You amuse me more and more.

VIVIANE (*definitely drunk*).   But that's marvellous! I should so like you to . . . like you to . . . (*Suddenly on the verge of tears*) I don't have to ask you to forgive me, but I'd like to ask you to.

BRIGITTE (*terribly touched*).   Viviane, my dear, you are . . . surprising.

VIVIANE.   You've made me drink too much.

BRIGITTE.   I've had too much too. A happy thought, perhaps, in one way . . .

VIVIANE.   If what makes a man happy made women happy too . . . but that's too much to ask.

BRIGITTE.   That won't happen tomorrow!

VIVIANE (*in a state of exaltation*).   And why not? We should be able to share out our joy all round us, to everyone, like bread. Why isn't that possible? . . . I suppose it's because we don't love anyone enough. And because even our happiness is rotten. And our love . . . mine, yours and Pierre's . . . is basically extremely selfish because it isn't real love.

BRIGITTE.   Now you're starting to talk like St John of the Cross!

VIVIANE (*almost a saint*).   Brigitte, may I kiss you? (VIVIANE *suits the action to the word.* BRIGITTE *pulls sharply away.*)

BRIGITTE.   We are making ourselves quite ridiculous, you know, the two of us!

GHOST (*to the audience*).   Utterly ridiculous!

VIVIANE.   Ridiculous in whose eyes? The spirits of the dead? . . . If circumstances had been different . . .

BRIGITTE.   If the circumstances had been different, I think I'd have liked to have you as my friend.

VIVIANE (*lighting up*).   Really?

BRIGITTE.   Whereas normally I have a marked preference for
  masculine friends.
VIVIANE.   Me too. (*A slight pause.*)
BRIGITTE.   Me too. You mean that you would have liked to be
  my friend, or that it's men who interest you?
VIVIANE.   Both . . . You've given me too much to drink!
  (*Holding out her glass to* BRIGITTE) But in the state I'm in now!
BRIGITTE.   In the state *we're* in now! (*She pours out whisky for*
  VIVIANE *and takes hold of the other bottle. Filling up her own*
  glass) I'm having gin.
VIVIANE.   It's lucky there's still some difference between us!
  (*They both laugh. Raising her glass*) Skol!
BRIGITTE.   Skol! (*They drink.*)
GHOST.   We welcome here tonight.
  The Minister for Suburban Technology.
  The Right Reverend Bishop Blank.
  The Equatorial Commissioner.
  Monsieur Gross the Means Test Recorder.
  Monsieur Net the Tax-Inspector.
  That's it:
  Monsieur Net the Tax-Inspector.
  Madame this . . .
  Madame that . . . Madame . . . What?
(*Overcome, he buries his head in his hands.*)
BRIGITTE (*as a great shiver runs over her*).   Brrrrr!
VIVIANE (*suffering from waves of heat*).   Poooooh!
BRIGITTE (*composing herself*).   Would you like me to put on a
  record? Pierre has just presented me with the complete recording
  of the Sonatas of Brezhnev played by . . . (*together*) Abraham
  Reisenberg.
VIVIANE.   Magnificent. A perfect example of that type of music.
  Pierre has just given me the two-record album
  Philippot's have just brought out.
BRIGITTE.   Poor Pierre! He eats double, he sees double. He hears
  double. And he buys double too . . . No wonder he's getting fat!
  (*The* GHOST *breathes out violently.*)
VIVIANE.   You can go on listening to music for ever, I'm glad to say.
  Beethoven, for example. You can still hear people on radio and
  television talking about his symphonies as if it was the first they'd
  ever heard—even the Ninth. But with a play, or a film . . . (*knowing*
  the answer is affirmative) You saw that one, of course: 'The
  Robot's Fiancé'? Pierre told me he'd taken you, the day before I
  went with him to see it—but not in the same cinema.
GHOST.   'The Robot's Fiancé'!!
BRIGITTE.   'The Robot's Fiancé' . . . That was with James Croning?
VIVIANE.   James Croning and Dorothy Burroughs.
BRIGITTE.   She's marvellous, Dorothy Burroughs. I adore her.

VIVIANE.   James Croning isn't bad either!
BRIGITTE.   Quite extraordinary. But I find in that role,
Dorothy Burroughs . . .
VIVIANE.   I couldn't agree with you more. It's definitely her finest
part.
BRIGITTE.   That scene when the Robot turns human—if that's the
right way to put it—and all his mechanism goes beserk, all those
bolts falling off, one by one, whimpering like a baby . . . While
she, on the other hand, sort of solidifies and gets transformed into
a statue made of flesh, horrible, threatening, staring straight out
with that vitriolic look . . .
VIVIANE (*sharing her lover's wife's enthusiasm*).   And the moment
when they're surrounded by the monkeys!
BRIGITTE.   Was that before or after?
VIVIANE.   Before.
BRIGITTE.   Oh yes! All those monkeys in uniform, brandishing
the Bible?
VIVIANE.   Yes, that's it, beating their chests with the other fist, as
if they were declaiming their sins.
BRIGITTE.   I must say I didn't quite go with that. That sequence
seemed to me a bit . . . a bit . . . too forced.
VIVIANE.   Not if you put it in its context. In all Peter Crosswell's
films there's always a moment when everything turns crazy, when
he goes in for the baroque. Don't forget he once came from Central
Europe.
BRIGITTE.   I know, but he's always lived in Paris.
VIVIANE.   It's in his blood. Baroque, rococo, bad taste—let's not be
afraid to admit it—it's an essential part of the world he creates. Do
you know one of his first films: 'When Twilight Meets the Dawn'?
I forget the title in French.
BRIGITTE. No, I don't know that one.
VIVIANE (*stretching her hand out towards the* GHOST).   May I burn
in hell if you're not crazy about it . . . they show it sometimes at
the Ciné Club. We could see it together? (*Realizing the
incongruousness of her proposition*) Good God! I forgot.
BRIGITTE.   So did I . . .
VIVIANE.   We go chattering on . . . (*Holding out her glass*) I'm
having whisky.
GHOST.   We welcome here tonight
The Minister for Suburban Technology.
And Monsieur, Monsieur
Monsieur Net the Tax-Inspector, that's it!
Madame . . . the Lady President of the Orgasms for All Club.
General this or
General that . . .
Crash! Bang! Wallop! Tit for tat
The General's flat!

BRIGITTE (*out of the blue*).   Shall we dance?
VIVIANE (*quite astonished*).   Dance!!
BRIGITTE.   Yes, I love dancing, don't you?
VIVIANE (*hesitantly*).   Yes . . . enormously . . .
BRIGITTE.   I can never dance with my husband.
VIVIANE.   Neither can I. I mean, with Pierre. He can't stand it!
  (*The* GHOST *starts to dance, lovingly clasping his briefcase
  in his arms.*)
BRIGITTE.   You set my mind at rest. I was afraid that with
  you . . .
VIVIANE.   No, no. Word of honour. (*Suddenly exhilarated*)
  Brigitte, you're sensational! Really tough! . . . O.K., let's dance!
  (BRIGITTE *is already by the record-player, selecting music.*) For
  each of us it'll be like piloting a bit of Pierre around. God, what
  am I saying?
BRIGITTE (*reading a record sleeve*).   'No Man's Land', what do
  you say to that?
VIVIANE.   Something slow. My head feels like a sponge . . . a good
  old slow one, for example, a slow foxtrot . . .
BRIGITTE (*searching through her records*).   A slow fox-trot . . .
  back to the Crimean War . . . Here we are! I think I've found one.
  (*She puts the record on. The two women listen to the opening
  bars.*)
VIVIANE.   Eureka! Ad hoc. Hic . . . (*She hiccups.*) . . . cup! Ma non
  troppo.

BRIGITTE *holds her arms out to* VIVIANE. VIVIANE *presses
herself against* BRIGITTE. *They dance. They dance slowly, clasping
each other closely, almost on the same spot. At one moment*
VIVIANE *will lean her face against* BRIGITTE's. *The* GHOST
*watches the two women as they dance. However, now revealing
great astonishment, which will seem comic to the audience, he
speaks.*

GHOST.   No, no! This is impossible!
  It's quite impossible, General!
  Where are we?
  Where am I?
  Fly away steering-wheel.
  Fly away Vivi
  Fly away Bridge . . .

  Suffer the little birds to come unto me
  Suffer the little birds to come unto me . . .

  The policeman has my car moved to the lay-by:
  'Your papers! Identification!'
  Surname, first name, occupation.
  And your treason permit.

I'm a corpse, I admit,
Constable, I became a corpse today,
Fresh and sweet as sage
And new-mown hay . . .
At your age!
Clear off then and move away!

The sky's in fragments, upside down
A gigantic landscape, quite distinct
Of stars extinct
Whose weary rounds leave their traces in my frown.
(*Surprised*.)
Who's this? Great-uncle with his watch of gold
And all his dignity gone cold.
And look now! Mr. Acknowledgement!
(*In conversation with a ghost*)
Nice day, Mr. Acknowledgement, today.
How does your offspring grow?
From the bottom up. As soon as I turn my back.
Still bottoms up, you know.
It doesn't do to be slack. Smack! Smack!
The very best of health!
You need all your wits about you . . .
Yes, Mr. Acknowledgement, you do,
Unless you're the Grand Vizier himself . . .
Well, you just stand your ground.
And remember me to your basset-hound.

No Man's Land:
A fog you could cut with a flaming brand
Fiery embers of horses must
First into ashes turn, then dust . . .
(*Pleading with the audience*)
Friends, brothers,
You thousands of shadowy ghouls
You thousands of blazing fools
You thousands of limbless eggs
With your wings folded under your legs
Blood-brothers in adversity
Half-brothers in perversity
Take pity on a nice fresh corpse!
(*Holding out his hat, as though begging for alms*)
A few pence for today
A few pence for today
So as not to go back to my hole straightaway . . .
A few pence for today
A few sous, a few dimes
So I can get dressed up to the nines . . .

(The slow fox-trot. The two women are dancing slowly right
beside him, then they move away.)
No Man's Land . . .
Here's Karl Marx, and George Sand
And little Jesus off to school. It's true . . .
And souls in the flesh, a kindly crew,
And scarlet elephants by the herd
—I dare not move or breathe a word—
And someone who looks like someone you mustn't ask
If he's the Man in the Iron Mask
Who's washing his hands in a bucket of sparks.
Gogol!
And dwarfs like bands of Mongols
And glaze-eyed soldiers barer than deserted parks

Three popes on skis, all
Off to have a ball.
And there, from the empty waste
Who's that coming my way in dreadful haste?
Who's that . . .
(Polite, but terrified)
No, no, I'm not here yet
You can see that I'm not here yet
I'm not in and I'm not out
My integration's not yet come about . . .
A little later if you like,
When I've had time to park my bike
And give a bone to Napoleone
Old Boney's got to have his boney.
Then I'll be back!
(He mops his brow, as though he had just escaped some frightful
danger.)
VIANE *(dancing).*   What time is he back from Orléans?
RIGITTE.   Tonight. You know that as well as I do!
VIANE.   Of course, I'm sorry.
HOST.   Drowned men in nightshirts seared
With fire. Bloody Bluebeard!
Hallo, bloody Bluebeard!
Just a minute, till I'm born
I'm not here yet
So half a tick
Give me the time to turn round and let
Me . . . camouflage the dawn
Give me the time to say Fiddlededee
Give me the time to say Old Nick . . .
A small boy who was once me
Is hopscotching off with my little silk hankee.
(To the child he was)

Hey there! Hey!
Too late
It's always too late
The dice are thrown
The chips are down . . .
(*In a familiar tone*)
A word of friendly advice
A tip from a patient, long-suffering fool:
Don't forget your folding-stool
'The protracted preparations for the Last Judgement
are still dragging on.'

Surname, First Name, Occupation.

A nice fresh corpse
A hundred mile-an-hour corpse
A full-steam-ahead corpse!

So many dead
So many dead on duty-practice
So many dead self-service
So many who still don't know they're dead
And so many more
Falling down into the sky galore . . .

Give me a penny, give me a sou
To turn me into a bugaboo . . .
(*Desperately hopeful*)
Is there anyone alive among you?
Alive enough
To want to breathe life up my nose?
. . . Then I'm sure I shall revive again!
I shall resuscitate
And expatiate
And wonder anew at the wild rose
And leavened bread's sweet freshness
Smiling at the eternal gentleness
Of milk, and at mankind's armour of bluff
Good-morning Mr. Cyclamen
Good-morning Mrs. Boniface
Good-day, amen, good-day, amen, good-day, amen
Then I shall wander, lively
Among the living dead and abide
In a fanfare of flesh and blood, and hide
My grim untimely grace
Good-day, amen, good-day, amen . . .
. . . My grim, untimely
Grace.
(*With a dying fall*)
Amen.

VIVIANE (*collapsing into the armchair next to the* GHOST).
 Phew! I'm drooping.
BRIGITTE (*also sitting down*). We're not used to it . . . One
 evening when I'd managed to drag Pierre off to do some
 dancing . . . (*Startled*) Do you notice a funny smell? . . . Like
 old leather or an old fur rug . . .
VIVIANE. Why, no, I can't smell anything at all. (*Sniffing*) Oh yes
 I can . . . But I'd say it was more like the scent of hawthorn or
 acacia . . . quite a long way off.
BRIGITTE. I'm getting less and less fond of this flat. I always told
 Pierre it was haunted.
VIVIANE. Haunted! That must have made him laugh! Pierre and
 the supernatural . . . (*A pause.*)
BRIGITTE. Don't you think the moment has come, Viviane, to
 have a serious talk?
VIVIANE. You are strange! We've done quite a lot of talking
 already.
BRIGITTE (*very gently*). Viviane, my dear Viviane . . . you are
 going to break it off, aren't you?
VIVIANE (*catching her breath*). Break it off! What on earth do
 you mean? Is that why you . . . Pierre and I love each other. And
 you've no right, you've no right at all . . . anyway, why should I
 be the one to . . .
BRIGITTE. Ssh! Ssh! Let's not get excited.
VIVIANE. I'm not excited.
GHOST (*after gathering himself together, shouting*). Beefsteak!
VIVIANE (*jumping*). Didn't you hear that shout?
BRIGITTE. Why, no.
VIVIANE (*very agitated*). I'm sure I heard someone shout.
GHOST (*as before, in great anguish*). Beefsteak! . . . (*To himself*)
 There are some words that just slip out . . . There's someone who
 . . . someone who draws the words out of my mouth . . . (*At the
 cost of enormous effort he again shouts out straight in front of
 him*) . . . Beefsteak!
VIVIANE. I'm positive!
BRIGITTE (*very quietly*). Viviane, Viviane, I'm talking to you
 quietly, without making a fuss, but deep down inside me I never
 stop shouting. It's me you're hearing.
VIVIANE. I'm absolutely positive. (*The telephone rings.* BRIGITTE
 goes to answer. The GHOST *and* VIVIANE *are now side by side,*
 VIVIANE *looking lovingly at the* GHOST) Petrov . . . Petrov,
 we will hang on to each other, won't we?
GHOST (*articulating energetically*). Hi-ma-la-ya. Himalaya.
BRIGITTE (*on the phone*). No, I won't hang up.
VIVIANE. What will become of me without you?
GHOST (*a prey to the words that trigger him off*). Laya . . . lafa . . .
 lafay . . . layette . . . layaf . . . after you . . . Af . . . Af . . . (*Facing*
 VIVIANE *and shouting*) . . . After you!

VIVIANE.   Such silence!

BRIGITTE (*out of patience*).   No, I won't hang up . . . I told you I was hanging on.

GHOST (*mangling his words, to* VIVIANE).   After you . . . you speak English? . . . Ich bin alt . . . Halte! Halte-là! Halt!

Silence. The GHOST *passes his hands over his face. Then he examines them as if they were two strange objects which no longer belonged to him, two puppets. He sits down on the floor, exhausted.*

BRIGITTE, *exceedingly nervy, is still waiting for the call to come through.*

Suddenly, the voice of SERGEANT LECOCQ *of the Gendarmerie is heard.*

SERGEANT'S VOICE (*with a regional accent*).   This is the Gendarmeri at Blancmange-sur-Taxe, Sergeant Lecocq.

BRIGITTE (*foreseeing the catastrophe*).   Sergeant Lecocq . . .

SERGEANT'S VOICE.   Is that Madame Freycinet?

BRIGITTE.   Yes, speaking.

SERGEANT'S VOICE.   Is your car a Mercedes SJ 3588 RQ?

BRIGITTE.   Yes. RQ. What's happened?

SERGEANT'S VOICE.   Well, you see . . . it's abaht your 'usband Freycinet, Pierre Freycinet, is that 'im?

BRIGITTE.   Yes, my husband . . .

The GHOST *greatly interested, has risen and goes to pick up the additional earphone.*

SERGEANT'S VOICE.   Pierre Freycinet 'as just 'ad an accident.

BRIGITTE.   Oh God!

SERGEANT'S VOICE.   On the Orléans road, not far from Blancmange There's a bend, and a tree. 'E ran into the tree. Speeding.

BRIGITTE.   Is it serious?

SERGEANT'S VOICE.   Well, you know . . . better come straight away, you know.

The GHOST *lays the earphone down on the table and moves away like a child who has been caught doing something wrong. But his face also reveals a kind of mischievousness, giving the impression that he is pleased with the little trick he has played.*

BRIGITTE.   He's not dead?

SERGEANT'S VOICE.   Well, you know . . . be in your own interest to come straight away, wouldn't it? 'E's in the 'ospital at Petits Fours.

BRIGITTE (*quite deflated*).   Petits Fours?

SERGEANT'S VOICE.   Yes, Petits Fours. Like the biscuits. You'll find 'im in Emergency, Abelard Ward.

BRIGITTE.   Abelard Ward . . . Was he asking for me?

SERGEANT'S VOICE. I can't 'ear you. What's that?

BRIGITTE. Did he ask for his wife? (*Silence.*) Was it his wife he was asking for?

SERGEANT'S VOICE. · Well, you know . . . Can't 'ardly say, being as 'ow 'e were found in a coma. Be in your interest to come straight away, wouldn't it?

BRIGITTE. Right, I'm on my way. Thanks.

SERGEANT'S VOICE. You're welcome.

VIVIANE (*who has instinctively registered the drama*). Something's happened to Pierre!

BRIGITTE (*opening a cupboard with several coats and putting one of them on*). Yes, a car accident.

VIVIANE. Serious?

BRIGITTE. Yes.

VIVIANE. Oh God! Where is he?

BRIGITTE. In the hospital at Petits Fours. I'm going at once. (*She has banged a hat on her head in haste.*)

VIVIANE. Petits Fours. I'm coming with you.

BRIGITTE (*cuttingly*). You're joking!

VIVIANE. Don't be silly. (*She puts her coat on. The* GHOST *mimes the movements for helping her.*)

BRIGITTE (*to herself*). The gas is off, the fridge is still switched on . . . Napoleon's still got something to eat, yes? . . . Yes . . . my keys. (*She opens her handbag and takes out her keys. To* VIVIANE) I'm not being silly, I'm his wife.

VIVIANE. Brigitte! (*Very humbly*) What if you were in my place?

BRIGITTE (*hard*). He wants me at his bedside.

VIVIANE (*distraught*). He . . . asked . . . for you . . .

BRIGITTE. Yes. He asked particularly for me. I'll keep you posted. You go first.

VIVIANE. You've got my private telephone number?

BRIGITTE. Of course.

VIVIANE. I'll be in all the time. You can call me at any hour.

BRIGITTE. Yes, you go first.

VIVIANE. At least I can take you to the station?

BRIGITTE. If you like.

The door closes behind the two women. The GHOST *remains alone on the stage. His face lights up. He taps out a few dance steps, appearing quite relieved at the disappearance of his two women. And now snatches of confused sounds reach him from outside: unarticulated sounds, bits of incomprehensible conversation—then, quite clearly this time, rising above the noises from the street, come the voices of* VIVIANE *and* BRIGITTE.

BRIGITTE (*Off, panting*). But where the hell *did* you park your car?

VIVIANE (*Off. More than miserable*). I thought it was somewhere here . . .

BRIGITTE (*Off*).   Rue Camembert, you told me just now.
VIVIANE (*Off*).   I never said that! It was you who mentioned the
    Rue Camembert.
BRIGITTE (*Off. Hailing a taxi*).   Hey! Hey! Taxi . . . taxi!
VIVIANE (*Off. Quite defeated*).   You'll phone me . . .

Screech of tyres. A car door slams. Noise of the taxi starting off.
The distant sound of a fire engine's siren. Silence.

GHOST.   The Minister of Suburban Technology
    The Right Reverend Bishop Blank
    Monsieur Gross the Means Test Recorder
    My mother Jezebel
    The Commissioner for Malicoco
    And Co, and Co, and Co . . .
(*To the audience, already aware of a different reality*)
    I am not Pierre!
    I am not . . . Petrov!

Very slight pause. He snaps his fingers, magically restarting the music
of the slow fox-trot. For a brief moment he inspects himself in the
mirror, then plucks a rose out of space. He puts the rose in a vase near
his portrait. He doffs his hat very slowly to his portrait. Then, he turns
to face the audience and, hat in hand, as if begging for alms, he
murmurs.

GHOST.   A few pence for today . . . a few pence for today . . .

With the other hand he has picked up his briefcase and his folding
stool.

And so, without haste and to the accompaniment of the music,
VIVIANE's *lover and* BRIGITTE's *husband, merged into one and*
the same person, disappears through the wall.

CURTAIN

THE BABY-SITTER

A Psychosomatic Comedy

Preface

Thirteen years of married bliss
But where are those Bengal lights I miss?!

Such is the *leitmotiv* frequently intoned by Elvira and Franklin, a
modern version of the eternal married couple of comedy. When the
curtain rises, they are both seen sprawling in their armchairs in the
interminable process of waiting. They are expected for dinner by
their friends, the Panicoffs, but they are stuck there at home, unable
to leave: the baby-sitter they have been counting on to keep an eye
on their children has failed to turn up.

Lassitude, bad temper and the acknowledged grievances each
harbours against the other slowly come to the surface. Franklin more-
over is suffering from a 'baby-sitter complex', a feeling of frustration
deriving, as he tells his wife, from the fact that as soon as one of these
ravishing young creatures bursts into his home, he is at once obliged
to make for the door and quit the premises. . . So when we sneak up
on the couple, time for them has been suspended.

But what of their life together over the last few years? Has it not
been a long succession of such moments? Where has it all gone, the
joy and the pregnant moments they shared when they were first
united?

At last the doorbell rings. But the baby-sitter does not turn out
to be quite the person they were waiting for . . . And the
confrontation that takes place between Elvira and Franklin and the
new arrival will give an unexpected twist to their relationship with
each other.

Characters

ELVIRA	Franklin's wife. About 30
FRANKLIN	Elvira's husband. Getting on for 40.
SISTER THORN OF THE HOLY GHOST	A bringer of good tidings.

Note

SILVER THORN OF THE HOLY GHOST can be played by a delightful
young virgin, vehemently inspired with zeal, or by a young woman the
same age as ELVIRA. She has obviously never known and never will know
any husband save Him who is in Heaven.

La Baby-Sitter was first performed on the 22nd of November 1971 at
the *Théâtre de l'Oeuvre* in a production by Pierre Franck. Décor by
Jacques Noël.

Scene One

A modest living-room, extremely cluttered. It is only too apparent that the occupiers have insufficient space.
When the curtain rises, ELVIRA and her husband FRANKLIN are each sprawled in an armchair.
She is in evening dress. He is wearing a lounge suit, or maybe a dinner jacket.
One should feel that there has been a long period of waiting.
Bad temper has taken a firm hold on both of them, but it will be more apparent in FRANKLIN. A long, long, long silence.

FRANKLIN.   Where's that bloody bitch got to?
ELVIRA.   She really is overdoing it. (*Looking at her wristwatch.*) More than half an hour late. (*A dangerous silence.*)
FRANKLIN.   Mind you, for all the fun we'd have been having at the Panicoffs.
ELVIRA (*irritated*).   Stay here, if you want to. No one's forcing you to go to the Panicoffs!
FRANKLIN.   Now I've taken the trouble to dress . . .

For the ninth time ELVIRA empties the contents of one handbag into another handbag, which is almost identical. She still doesn't know which one to choose.

ELVIRA.   There was a time when you swore by the Panicoffs.
FRANKLIN.   Once upon a time . . . my grandmother had her own teeth!
ELVIRA.   If it puts you in a mood like this . . . (*A pause*)
FRANKLIN.   Who'll be there at the Panicoffs, apart from us?
ELVIRA.   Olga mentioned the Brenners, the Martinettes, the Ouglies, the Traveltours and possibly Doctor Cameroun, if he's not on call . . . Oh! I was forgetting: Madame or Monsieur Bloch is meant to be coming too. Since the separation they each take it in turns. If it's not Madame, it's her 'late' husband.
FRANKLIN.   The same old faces, eh!
ELVIRA.   I've told you, if you don't want to go . . . you can keep an eye on the children instead . . . Personally, *I* always enjoy dinner at the Panicoffs.
FRANKLIN.   Oh you, so long as you get a good blow-out . . .
ELVIRA.   May I gently remind you, *my dear,* that at the Panicoffs the food is always awful. Olga, when it comes to cooking . . .

And if there's one of us who likes to make a pig of himself,
it's certainly not me!

FRANKLIN. Well, that's a new line, I must say! I make a pig
of myself, do I?

ELVIRA. It's quite obvious. When you're eating, no one gets a peep
out of you. You just vanish into your stomach. (*A slight pause.*)

FRANKLIN. It's true that when I find myself in front of a table
covered with goodies and I think about all the starving millions
in the Third World . . .

ELVIRA. Oh, it's an intellectual pastime, is it?

FRANKLIN. You can poke fun at me, but in fact, when I do
justice to my food, I have the impression I'm engaged in a serious
occupation.

ELVIRA. I admit no one could say you make light of your stomach.
And when it's over, you ruminate.

FRANKLIN. I ruminate! I ruminate!

ELVIRA. Why, think of last time at the Panicoffs. There were just
the four of us—I felt quite ashamed, the way you gobbled up those
artificial eggs, the beefsteak mousse, and that cream of Jerusalem
artichokes. Never a word from you all through dinner. Then you
settled into an armchair and never opened your mouth again!

FRANKLIN. What do you expect me to say to the Panicoffs? I have
nothing, nothing to say to the Panicoffs.

ELVIRA. You might at least be polite and pretend you had.

FRANKLIN. Robert's an encyclopaedia, he knows everything. As
for Olga, the best you can say for her is that she's eminently
screwable. But as I can't in all decency screw her in front of you . . .

ELVIRA. Franklin, you're impossible. Especially when you're hungry!

FRANKLIN (*following up his idea*). And after all, one can't help
wondering why? Where is the code of morals that forbids it?
What's its longitude? And what about 'latitude'?

ELVIRA. Oh no! You're not going back on that old communal
marriage track again!

FRANKLIN. All right, all right . . . (*With a martyred air*) We'll come
up to date. (*A pause.*) What's that bloody bitch of a baby-sitter up
to? It's twenty to nine already, and it takes at least an hour to find
their wretched suburban bungalow.

ELVIRA. Three quarters of an hour, if that.

FRANKLIN. Including the wrong turnings? Nothing looks more like
a suburban bungalow than another suburban bungalow.

ELVIRA. We've been there fifteen times at least!

FRANKLIN. Not so long ago, that didn't stop you marching me into the
house of a family of half-wits.

ELVIRA. Because of the fog. There was such a fog that evening!

FRANKLIN. Talk about making an entrance! I'll never forget it.
There they were, all round that table, leaping to their feet as
one man. (*Imitating a man with a gravelly voice*) 'Who the hell do

you think you are? Inspectors from Social Security . . .' The man
we took to be dad just came up to my waist. The nine children
all round him were each of them nine foot tall, and the mother
cast ostrich-eyes at me . . . And then that legless wonder? . . .
Appearing out of nowhere on stilts! . . . And me backing out: sorry,
je m'excuse . . . où est la maison de M. Panicoff? . . . Pardon . . .
sorry . . . je m'excuse . . .

ELVIRA.   Ssh! . . . wasn't that Pascal? . . . Unless it was Véronique.
(*Silence.*) I'll go and listen behind their door . . .

ELVIRA *leaves the room.* FRANKLIN *makes for the cocktail
cabinet with great rapidity.*

FRANKLIN (*alone*).   I'm jumping the gun, jumping the gun! (*Opens
the cabinet, takes out the sugar bowl and pours almost half its
contents into his pocket. He sits down again in his armchair
crunching a lump of sugar.*) Keep going! You've got to keep
going! . . . Come to my aid, you glucosides, while I wait for the
proteins, the lipids, and the Danaides with their leaky vessel . . .
Keep going!

　　　Thirteen years of conjugal bliss
　　　But where are those Bengal lights I miss?!
(*A pause.*) Oh God, I'm fed up! I'm fed up! I don't know exactly
why, but I'm fed up. And I'm fed up with being fed up! . . .
To start with, this flat's too small. Now, with Pascal and
Véronique growing and growing, getting fatter and fatter all
the time . . . And the higher they climb, the flatter they fall,
that's mathematics. Especially the little chap. Ever since he
got that landing-strip for Boeing 909's . . . Hell! What I need
now is someone to make me a present of Orly Airport! Keep
going. Behave as if I was really me! (*A pause. He crunches
another lump of sugar. Then stands up, looks at himself
in the glass, and pulls a face. Taking off* ELVIRA's *way of
speaking*) May I gently remind you, *my dear,* that you're
looking more and more like your mother: those lines at the
corner of your mouth, those old bag eyes, the same wrinkle
between the eyebrows, that vertical one . . . not exactly dishy!
How exasperating Elvira can be! She cuts me down to size.
She spends her time cutting me down to size . . . furious
because I'm not the person she thought I was when I seemed to
be a person I wasn't . . . it's two other people who get married,
two other people who swear to be faithful. Everyone's committed
but you. The old old story! . . . One ought to marry an animal: a
tortoise, a donkey, a goldfish . . . (*Ecstatically*) Meet the tortoise
of your life . . . Grow old together, very slowly . . . (*In his party
voice*) Luckily, there are the children! . . . You said it! Children
are little ogres. It's our children who gobble us up. Yes, that's
it! . . . With pockets full of little white pebbles . . . The cannibals

appear to have devoured their children in their infancy. Of course, that's why there are no more cannibals: it's the price you pay for consuming your own posterity . . . (*He swallows another lump of sugar.*) A two-storey flat. That's what I need. a two-storey flat. With me occupying all the upper floor. And the family groaning at my feet. And a young student as au pair girl . . . (*Subtly*) For dad, *au père*! Curvetting, besetting, upsetting . . . And it goes without saying that if I was properly installed, I wouldn't go out so much to other people. The Panicoffs could go and get stuffed . . . I'd entertain myself, I'd invite myself to dinner . . . (*Rising from his armchair and appearing to greet his best friend*) Tiens, Franklin, comment ça va? . . . (*He shakes himself by the hand.*) Comment ça va? . . . (*The same business each time*) Comment ça va? . . . Comment ça va? . . . Comment ça va? Eh bien, alors! . . . C'est l'heure de se mettre à table . . . Eh bien! J'attends. J'attends toujours . . . (*He suddenly falls sprawling into his armchair as he hears* ELVIRA's *footsteps approaching.*)

ELVIRA. Oh! those neighbours and their telly!

FRANKLIN. What about the brats, then?

ELVIRA. Sound asleep. Clenching their little fists.

FRANKLIN. Clenching their fists! Already! Like regular little strikers!

ELVIRA (*very pityingly*). Very funny . . . (*Slight pause.*) Franklin, shall we slip away without making a sound? Once they've gone to sleep . . .

FRANKLIN. No, no! Suppose Véronique has a nightmare and wakes up calling for her daddy!

ELVIRA. May I gently remind you, my dear, that Véronique never calls for her daddy. She always calls for her mummy! For that matter, so does Pascal.

FRANKLIN (*wearily*). Obviously.

ELVIRA. What do you mean, obviously? It's a fact. (*A rather long pause.*)

FRANKLIN. And what of the time she called for Gaston?

ELVIRA. Gaston?

FRANKLIN. A little mite who's only just turned seven! Perhaps Gaston was really you too?

ELVIRA. Franklin, you're being utterly ridiculous!

FRANKLIN. Oh, I see, I'm being ridiculous because I heard her calling for one of those little gigolos at school.

ELVIRA. I prefer not to answer . . . (*A pause.*) If you're so terribly hungry, eat a lump of sugar. (FRANKLIN *starts barking. The telephone rings.* ELVIRA *picks up the receiver.*) Hello, yes . . . I . . . I . . . I . . . I (ELVIRA *tries to get a word in, but her caller obviously refuses to give her a chance. Finally*) What you're saying, Monsieur, is extremely . . . extremely . . . erotic. But you've made a mistake, I am not Charlotte . . . No, I'm not offended, not at this distance . . . I'm sorry? She told you

she'd be here at this time? She ought to be here at this time?
She ought to be here, that's true. We're waiting for her . . .

FRANKLIN.   J'attends toujours.

ELVIRA.   Can I give her a message?

FRANKLIN.   That takes the biscuit!

ELVIRA.   . . . But there's no need to blush, young man.
(FRANKLIN *jumps with surprise. Covering the receiver with one
hand and whispering to her husband*) Some poor spotty youth,
I can just imagine him! . . . (*To her caller*) How old are you?
(ELVIRA *is visibly amused*.) Fifteen . . . and you're working
for your Union's A-level Certificate! . . . What's your first
name? . . . (*She hangs up*.) . . . He hung up.

FRANKLIN.   That really is the limit! If you're going to play
secretary for your baby-sitter! (*The telephone rings*.) Again!

ELVIRA (*having picked the receiver up again*). Hello . . .
Eugène? . . . What number did you want, Monsieur? . . . Yes,
that's right . . . Hello . . . (*She hangs up*.) That one hung up
straight away.

FRANKLIN.   Eugène! A Rumanian, what's more! . . . Just think of
it! We're no sooner out of our flat and it's converted into a
brothel! . . . And on top of that we have to pay her Union rates.
I do, that is. Not those little layabouts who come poking their
way up here, wave after wave of them.

ELVIRA.   No need to exaggerate. They've not done too much
damage as yet. Apart from your solid ivory cuff links, your
planisphere and your collection of cameras . . .

FRANKLIN.   A trifle . . . a flea-bite . . . and when it comes to
drugs.

ELVIRA.   What are you on about now?

FRANKLIN.   When we came home last time, didn't you notice
a funny smell?

ELVIRA.   Nothing at all.

FRANKLIN.   I know your baby-sitters!

ELVIRA.   If your mother deigned to come and keep an eye on her
grandchildren now and then . . .

FRANKLIN.   It's a long time since my mother did that!

ELVIRA.   You must admit it would save us a lot of money . . . A
woman with absolutely nothing to do who spends her time
imbibing alcohol in front of the television set.

FRANKLIN.   My mother detests children, you know that quite
well. She couldn't even keep a proper eye on me. I was premature.
A whole school term before my time.

ELVIRA.   Poor little chick! . . . You don't want a whisky while you
wait?

FRANKLIN.   On an empty stomach? What an idea! (*Almost begging*)
Unless there's a little cold veal left . . .

ELVIRA.   Not one morsel, the kids scoffed the lot.

FRANKLIN (*ominously*). All right, all right. That's just perfect.

ELVIRA.　Anyway, if you start eating now, you'll never be able to swallow a thing at the Panicoffs.

FRANKLIN.　The Panicoffs . . . (*Beating his fist*) But what's that bloody tart up to? . . . And by the way, who is it this evening?

ELVIRA.　Charlotte. You heard who it was.

FRANKLIN.　Oh yes! That plump little piece with great big dollipops. I can't stand that one. She looks like a parachutist. Why didn't you get hold of Dorothy, or Christine, or Pamela? Or why not that Swedish bit?

ELVIRA.　Viveca?

FRANKLIN.　Viveca. Now she's very pretty. Long blonde hair, and legs, and a skin . . . ! Have you noticed her skin?

ELVIRA.　Yes, very fresh. But she doesn't inspire me with confidence. Not like Charlotte.

FRANKLIN.　She's not a thief just because she's pretty!

ELVIRA.　I never said she was a thief. It's just that, if there was some little upset . . . the house on fire or the revolution starting, Charlotte wouldn't lose her cool. Whereas Viveca, once she's plunged into her porno magazines . . .

FRANKLIN (*excited*). What's that? I didn't know. Porno magazines?

ELVIRA.　The first time she came—I was meant to be meeting you at the Traveltours—she had a dozen of them under her arm at least. She just threw them down, nonchalantly, on the table. At first I thought they were exercise books. Trigonometry. But when I had a closer look . . . all those colour photos, with one on top of the other . . .

FRANKLIN.　Fascinating! Fascinating! And you didn't say anything to her?

ELVIRA.　You bet I did. I made a remark like: if the little boy gets up during the night and comes to ask for a glass of water, I wonder if you'd mind camouflaging all this!

FRANKLIN.　You're really very hard on Pascal!

ELVIRA.　I ask you, Franklin! I know in those Scandinavian countries they start their sexual education very young, but our poor little chap, who's only just five . . .

FRANKLIN.　In any case, if I had to choose between Viveca and Charlotte, I wouldn't hesitate. I much prefer Viveca.

ELVIRA.　Yes, but Pascal much prefers Charlotte.

FRANKLIN (*getting carried away*). At the ripe age of five, Pascal can hardly appreciate these matters as I can. You surely don't put Pascal's infantile gropings on the same plane as . . . as . . .

ELVIRA.　May I gently remind you, *my dear*, that even if Viveca did ring our doorbell this evening, it's not for your sake she'd be coming, but Pascal's.

FRANKLIN.　I must say, it's a terrible shame!

ELVIRA (*in some consternation*).　Franklin! . . . Anyone would think, to hear you, that you're frustrated, that . . .

FRANKLIN.   Frustrated. Yes and no. One's always frustrated
about something, every time you make a choice.

ELVIRA.   Obviously, I'm not eighteen any more. I'm really
sorry . . . But you're no spring chicken either, and to put it
bluntly I can't see Viveca panting with desire . . . to ring our
doorbell . . .

FRANKLIN.   Point taken, say no more. (*A very short pause.*)
All the same, I still prefer Viveca.

ELVIRA (*restraining herself*).   Besides, Franklin, may I gently
remind you that the very minute a baby-sitter enters this
room—whether it's Micheline, Viveca or Betty—you leave the
premises.

FRANKLIN.   Correct. Only too correct. Now you rub salt into
the wound. That's what's so frustrating. The fact that, the
very moment one of these ravishing creatures waltzes into my
home, I have to turn myself out of doors . . .

ELVIRA.   That's right!

FRANKLIN.   Whereas in other circumstances, in *normal* circumstances, Betty or Micheline, or Viveca would ask nothing
better than to establish contact with me, to exchange
pleasantries and profit from my experience of life.

ELVIRA (*more than teasing*).   No doubt!

FRANKLIN.   Discuss computer programming, or what have
you? . . . There are a *few* young people today who aren't
nihilists. There's a silent minority too, keen on improving
themselves, anxious to give themselves body—and soul— to
some noble cause, I'm sure of that!

ELVIRA.   You know you're getting to be quite a joke!

FRANKLIN.   Of course, for you the question is rather different.
(*Pause*) One evening I'll let *you* go out with the children, and
I'll let Viveca keep an eye on *me*.

Silence. ELVIRA'*s eyes pass right through her husband, right
through the furniture, right through the wall.*

ELVIRA.   I hope Dr. Cameroun will be there.

FRANKLIN.   Ah yes, why's that?

ELVIRA.   Because he has a colleague, one of his best friends,
who's a psychoanalyst. You can take his address. Perhaps
he'll be able to get rid of your obsessions, of your baby-
sitter complex.

FRANKLIN.   Complex! Big words all at once! My reaction's a
perfectly healthy one. A man's reaction. Nowadays there are
so few real men about that when a man has a man's attitude,
a primitive attitude, the whole tribe gets disturbed, the
tribe takes fright. That's it: the tribe takes fright. (*He takes
a lump of sugar from his pocket and swallows it.*)

ELVIRA.   You've emptied that sugar bowl again!

FRANKLIN.   Carbohydrates! . . . Keep going. Got to keep going!

ELVIRA AND FRANKLIN (*in the same tone*).
   Thirteen years of conjugal bliss.
   But where are the Bengal lights I miss?!

ELVIRA *paces nervously up and down the room.*

ELVIRA (*consulting her watch*).   This is getting most alarming.
FRANKLIN.   Perhaps something's happened to her. With those great tits.
ELVIRA.   She could have telephoned!
FRANKLIN.   Why don't you phone? She may have forgotten.
ELVIRA.   Charlotte's not on the telephone.
FRANKLIN.   I suppose we'd better warn the Panicoffs anyway, that
   we're still stuck here, tied hand and foot, walled up, nullified.
ELVIRA.   If she's not here in the next five minutes, I'll give Olga
   a ring.
FRANKLIN.   Better do it now. What if she's been preparing leg of
   lamb cooked in ashes or turkey stuffed with prunes . . .
ELVIRA.   I've no fears at all on that score!

ELVIRA *sits down again.* FRANKLIN *gets up and goes to the*
television set. He switches on, but the set fails to light up.

FRANKLIN.   That bloody set's conked out again . . . if only you'd
   stop our little lad always fiddling with the knobs . . . (FRANKLIN,
   getting more and more weary, sits down again, discouraged. Sighing)
   If I'd known, I'd have sat down with my Teach Yourself!
ELVIRA (*almost gaily*).   Have you taken up your English again?
   Your Italian, I mean.
FRANKLIN (*superior*).   English, Italian: dead languages! . . . (*He waits*
   for the effect to register.) My Chinese, if you really want to know.
ELVIRA.   Your Chinese! You're learning Chinese now?!
FRANKLIN.   And why shouldn't I learn Chinese? Haven't I the right
   to learn Chinese?
ELVIRA.   Don't be silly. But . . .
FRANKLIN.   You won't be sorry when we're invaded by those
   Maoists and I start talking Mao to them.
ELVIRA.   Poor Franklin!
FRANKLIN.   Poor Franklin! Poor Franklin! Can't you see it's exciting,
   anyway, to learn a new language? Still more, when hardly anyone
   speaks it.
ELVIRA.   Apart from eight-hundred-million Chinese.
FRANKLIN.   Apart from eight-hundred-million Chinese. You can be
   quite maddening, can't you! . . . Being one of the first to learn it,
   that's what's important . . . Imagine the first Congolese to speak
   Russian, strolling around Red Square and asking the Russians the
   way, in Russian! They must have been tickled pink—especially as
   the Russians are pretty racist! . . . A man as black as your hat from
   top to toe who starts reciting Pushkin, who stands with his hands in
   his pockets and talks Kolkhoz—must be shattering!

ELVIRA. And does it really exist, a Teach Yourself Chinese?

FRANKLIN. Underground. Top secret. You can bet your life the Chinese are far from anxious to let the Americans or the Ukranians learn the Chinese way of saying: my tailor is a rich man.

VERONIQUE (*Off*). Mummy! Mummy!

ELVIRA. Véronique! It's not my imagination this time.

VERONIQUE (*Off*). Mummy! Mummy! (*In tears.*)

FRANKLIN. You see, if we'd gone out by now . . . I'll go, stay where you are. (FRANKLIN *rushes off to the children's room.*)

ELVIRA (*alone*). Chinese! (*She opens the cabinet, takes out the whisky and drinks straight from the bottle. Then she looks at herself in the glass and inspects herself in detail, while humming*)

> Chinese night
> Oh night supine
> Oh Chinese night of love . . .
> . . . tum tee-tum tee-tum tee-tum
> . . . tee-tum tee-tum tum-tum
> Chinese night
> Oh night feline
> Oh night . . .

FRANKLIN (*bursting in*). The pot? Where did you put the pot?

ELVIRA (*taken aback*). What pot?

FRANKLIN. You know, the pot.

ELVIRA. Still in the same place, next to Teddy. Is that why she's crying?

FRANKLIN. Don't worry. (*He has already gone again.*)

ELVIRA. As soon as it's Véronique . . . if it was Pascal he wouldn't lift his little finger . . . (*Looking at her watch*) Almost nine o'clock. That girl's really overdone it! If she turns up, I've a good mind to send her packing. Well, perhaps not . . . (*She looks at herself in the glass again, pulling her face about.*) Of course, Members of the Court, Members of the Jury, I am not sixteen any more . . . To start with, it's such a stupid age to be, sixteen, so . . . so intermediate! Curious creatures, men: the more years they put on, the more they'd like their wives to take off . . . they ought to marry their daughters and be done with it. (*Imitating* FRANKLIN) I still prefer Viveca anyway . . . (*Standing back and aiming at her reflection in the mirror, as if she was holding a machine-gun*) Tac, tac, tac, tac, tac, tac, tac! (*She collapses onto the sofa, mortally wounded. Continuing her little act*) Ah! I'm dying! I'm dying! Help me! Charlotte, Micheline, Betty, Viveca, Ingrid, Lisbeth, Eugenie, give me your breasts, give me your belly, give me your buttocks firm. Give me this day your daily sex . . . Keep the old flag flying . . . (*Declaiming*) I am a woman who's growing old, withering away . . . My glamour is flaking off. Gather the pieces, travellers, in your trembling hands. And lay my shade to rest in the tomb of your desire. My navel shines no more, the sun of man's delight. It goes to ground in shame, like an animal in the night. Every evening one more life-line snaps. Swollen feet and thighs gone blue. Hurry, voyagers, before my fleece has turned to snow. The ravens will soon be here. I am a woman who's growing old and getting in the way . . . (*Suddenly sitting up straight, very naturally*) Which means Franklin's not such a catch now either!

She goes back to the bar and drinks a glass of whisky full to the brim. Slightly tight and brandishing the bottle.

Thirteen years of conjugal bliss
But where are the Bengal lights I miss?!

The telephone rings. She picks up the receiver.

. . . Yes, Monsieur, that's the number . . . No, Monsieur, I am not Charlotte . . . Yes, Monsieur, I am the lady of the house . . . No, thank you very much . . . No, Monsieur, I did not hit the ceiling because of what you said . . . No, Monsieur, I am not 'a game old girl' . . . (*She hangs up. The phone rings again almost at once. Picking up the receiver again*) . . . Hello, Albert? Good evening Albert. No, nothing nothing serious, we're waiting for the baby-sitter . . . Your guests are hungry? . . . Madame Bloch is yawning like a dormouse? Now I know why Monsieur Bloch left her! . . . (*She laughs.*) Yes, of course, don't wait for us, start without us . . . Olga's made a beetroot soufflé? Good God!! . . . Oh no, I'm not surprised, she's such a splendid cook . . . a soufflé, especially a beetroot one, we'll never be forgiven! (*The door bell rings.*) Ah! Victory at last! There's someone at the door. About forty minutes and we'll be there. Bye! (*She hangs up.*)

FRANKLIN (*who has just burst in, furious*). Why can't she stop ringing that bell. She'll wake the children. (*Shouts*) The key's in the lock. Don't move, I'm going to take your little tart by the ears and shake her till she squeals! (*He marches firmly to the door.*)

Scene Two

FRANKLIN (*opening the door*).   Bravo! Well done! Congratulations on getting here so early! . . . Oh, I'm sorry, Mademoiselle, you're not Charlotte!

A young girl—or a young woman—appears, quite pretty beneath that uniform—Salvation Army type—with a briefcase under her arm bursting with pamphlets and leaflets.

SISTER THORN (*presenting herself very stiffly*).   Sister Thorn of the
   Holy Ghost.
FRANKLIN (*bowing to the ground*).   My respects, Sister.
SISTER THORN.   I have come to bring you the good news.
ELVIRA (*whose surprise has now given way to happy excitement*).
   Good news is so rare nowadays. Come in, come in, make yourself
   at home!
FRANKLIN.   Yes do, please do, do come in, Sister!

*Husband and wife, suddenly discovering a source of entertainment,
exchange conspiratorial glances.*

SISTER THORN (*without budging an inch*).   Christ is risen.
FRANKLIN.   I know. We know. And he went up to Heaven. And has
   never been seen again.
ELVIRA.   Don't take any notice, Mademoiselle, my husband's very
   hungry. And when he's hungry he doesn't know what he's saying!
SISTER THORN.   Blessed are those who are hungry, for they shall be
   eaten!
FRANKLIN.   Blessed are those who are thirsty, for they shall be
   licked!
ELVIRA.   Franklin!
SISTER THORN.   Let your right cheek bless your left cheek.
FRANKLIN.   An eye for a tooth. A tooth for an eye.
SISTER THORN.   To the man who has wealth, I shall grant even
   more. To the man who has naught, I shall give even less.
FRANKLIN.   The first shall be last, and the last shall be least.
SISTER THORN.   Love your enemies.
FRANKLIN.   And hate your friends.
SISTER THORN.   Blessed are the poor in spirit.
ELVIRA.   Suffer the little children to come unto me. Please do,
   Mademoiselle, come inside! Don't just stand there the two of you,
   on the landing, bandying divinity with each other.
FRANKLIN.   My wife is right, Sister, plunge into the holy of holies . . .
ELVIRA.   We were just getting ready to leave, without actually going.
FRANKLIN (*happily*).   Yes, you've arrived at a perfect moment. Just
   when time was standing still, in a kind of no-man's-land of our
   domestic life.
SISTER THORN (*still very stiff*).   Time is dead for all sinners. It is
   quick for the children of light.
ELVIRA.   All the more reason not to stay there in the dark.

SISTER THORN *moves forward a few paces and inspects her
surroundings.*

FRANKLIN (*eagerly*).   *Venite*, Sister, *venite*.
ELVIRA.   It's not very big, our flat. But our heart's all there.
SISTER THORN.   In my Father's house are many mansions.
FRANKLIN (*pushing up a broad armchair*). Would you like this
   armchair, Sister?

SISTER THORN (*glacial*).   No, thank you, not that armchair.
(*Astonishment of* ELVIRA *and* FRANKLIN. *A pause.*) The two of
you have fornicated in that armchair. You have fornicated. And wors
(ELVIRA *turns away and bursts out laughing.*)

FRANKLIN (*playing indignation*).   Mademoiselle, I am the honourable
father of a family.

ELVIRA (*playing up in turn*).   And that's more than can be said of yo

FRANKLIN.   And that's more than can be said of you!

ELVIRA.   It's better to love and count the cost!

FRANKLIN.   Than never to have loved and lost!

SISTER THORN (*in a kind of ecstasy*).   Peace! Peace, lambkins! I was
not led here by the Holy Ghost in order to bury you beneath the
mountain of your misdeeds, but to deliver you and point out the way
to Kingdom Come . . . to the Realm of Omnipotence, to the Land of
Canaan.

FRANKLIN.   In that case, perhaps you'd prefer this chair? (ELVIRA ir
her corner has another fit of the giggles.) It belonged to my great-
uncle. He was a Locum Tenens.

SISTER THORN *sits down, with a very straight back. She places the
briefcase at her feet. She sits there on her chair without saying a word,
stiff as a poker.*

FRANKLIN.   Please make yourself comfortable, Sister. Relax a little.
Look on this house of sinners as an ineffable . . . (*Searching for the
words*) trespass . . .

ELVIRA (*Going to his rescue*).   . . . on the road to your deliverance.

FRANKLIN.   That's it!

SISTER THORN.   Pray accept my thanks.

ELVIRA.   Would you like a cushion?

SISTER THORN.   The Lord said: Keep an upright spine and your spirit
won't veer to the left. (*A pause.*)

FRANKLIN (*merely anxious to break the silence*).   Oh yes! The left,
the Left! . . . There's a lot to be said for the Left . . . (*A fresh silence.*
Darling, what if you offered our guest something, our seventh-hour
adventist?

ELVIRA.   But, of course. What would Sister like?

FRANKLIN.   Gin and tonic? Whisky? Vodka?

ELVIRA (*selecting the bottles*). Carpano? Vermouth? Bols? Triple
Dry?

SISTER THORN.   The Lord has forbidden us alcohol.

FRANKLIN.   I didn't know you and the Lord had a personal relationship. How is he at the moment?

SISTER THORN (*inspired*).   He is well. Very well. Extremely well.

FRANKLIN.   That's fine then, mighty fine.

SISTER THORN (*still inspired*).   He said to me: Go, my bleating ewe-
lamb, go thrust thyself into the wolf's lair . . . Let the wolf devour

thee, let his jaws close about thee, and thy fire shall burn into his vitals.

FRANKLIN. The wolf, that's me.

SISTER THORN (*joyfully*). You are the wolves!

FRANKLIN. And wolves, as is well-known, drink whisky. (*Accepting the glass of whisky* ELVIRA *is offering to him.*) Begging your pardon. (*He drinks.*)

ELVIRA. I'm the wolf's wife. (*She drinks.*)

SISTER THORN (*serenely*). St. Paul has written: 'So long as they dwelt in ignorance, so long as they knew not the Law, they lived not in sin . . . Now that they know the Law, woe to them if they transgress it, for then they shall commit sinfulness, and the right hand of the Lord shall bear down upon them, and they shall be cast into Gehenna!'

ELVIRA. For Heaven's sake, whatever you do, don't acquaint us with the Law! (*She drinks.*)

SISTER THORN. All men have been sent into the world to learn the Law of the Lord, and to observe it and embrace His Rule. (*Getting up and singing in a ferrety voice*)

>Your impenetrable Ways, oh Lord,
>Pierce us through and through.
>And our wicked flesh, oh Lord,
>Adorns the heart of You.
>Hosannah! Hosannah!
>I'm waving Heaven's banner,
>Hosannah! Hosannah!
>Misericordia.

FRANKLIN. Bravo!

ELVIRA. Sublime!

SISTER THORN (*Quietly*).

>You swoop like a hawk out of space
>On our chaste pleasures here below,
>Your Rule we dutifully embrace
>From which our Dignity doth flow.
>Hosannah! Hosannah! I'm waving Heaven's banner . . .

ALL THREE (*in chorus*).

>Hosannah! Hosannah!
>Misericordia.

FRANKLIN. Our young pop stars can pack their bags! (*Raising his glass of whisky*) You're sure you won't . . . Right, O.K. Here's health to those who have none. (*He drinks.*)

ELVIRA (*raising her glass*). To ignorance! (*She empties her glass in one gulp.*)

SISTER THORN (*gently compassionate*). Is that something to rejoice and boast about? . . . Is it a privilege not to understand one's own nature? Can we be flattered, Madame, by the thought that we are mere animals?

ELVIRA (*unctuously*). Very often, Sister, the animal in us protects us from the man.

SISTER THORN. A man, Madame, is far more than a man.

FRANKLIN (*drink on an empty stomach making him dangerously eloquent*). I wear myself out telling her that! Take me, for example, your husband. (*To* SISTER THORN) Yes, you have in front of you something that's called a husband—well, I'm far more than a mere married man. Far more than you think. (*He drinks.*)

SISTER THORN. And far more than even *you* think, Monsieur. All our Father's creatures are diamonds, diamonds dipped in darkness.

ELVIRA. That's very beautiful, what you just said!

SISTER THORN (*in raptures*). And though each one is different, they all shine the same. Examine leaves from a tree under a microscope and you notice that none are alike. So do you each have your own peculiarities. Yet you are all attached to the branches of the same tree. You rustle, you twitter. (*Carried away by her own verbosity*) You pear, you apple, you cherry, you acorn, you apricot, you . . . you extrafoliate!

FRANKLIN (*who is highly amused, to* ELVIRA). Isn't it Plato, to be precise, who compares man to a tree? (*To* SISTER THORN) A tree that grows upside down.

SISTER THORN (*gently*). Plato, Monsieur, is a gentleman of small importance.

FRANKLIN. I don't doubt it. I was quoting Plato as I might have quoted . . .

SISTER THORN. A small boy.

ELVIRA. Like my husband, believe me. Every morning I have to give him a wash and brush up, comb his hair, dress him, tie his shoe-laces and pack him off to the office—just like a small boy.

FRANKLIN. A small boy that brings back the lolly.

ELVIRA. Peanuts. No ambition. When he asks for an increase, it's through my mouth he speaks. If I didn't push him . . .

SISTER THORN. Who shall increase in this world shall by so much diminish in the next. Ephesians 8:24.

FRANKLIN (*jubilant*). That's it! There's the argument I've been looking for for thirteen years! Oh, thank you, Sister. Whosoever loveth his reward, shall lose it!

SISTER THORN (*with the joy of a Communist meeting another member of the Party*). Ephphatha! Ephphatha! Yes. Now you've said it. And whosoever loseth his reward shall gain it. Ephphatha! (*To* ELVIRA) Do the birds in the Heavens, Madame, give thought to their daily bread?

ELVIRA (*irritated*). *Do* they! They do nothing but, morning, noon and night.

FRANKLIN. They pretend they do, to keep up appearances.

ELVIRA. Sister, have you ever really looked at the eye of a bird? There's nothing more voracious than a bird's eye.

SISTER THORN (*nothing it seems can put her out of countenance*). When you look at a bird, the bird looks at you with a different eye.

A bird's eye that eyes you, sees the eyes of a killer. Do you eat chicken, Madame?

ELVIRA. No more than I have to. All chickens nowadays taste of mackerel.

SISTER THORN. When I say chicken, I *think* winged creature. I could just as well have said: quail, partridge, willow-warbler, thrush, lark . . . (*Ecstatically*) Larks! Every morning an exaltation!

FRANKLIN (*flapping his wings*). Cui, cui, cui, cui, cui, cui, cui, cui.

ELVIRA. Franklin.

SISTER THORN. Nature turned into the enemy of man because man became unnatural. Once he rejected his primordial state, once he . . . (*Telephone rings.*)

FRANKLIN (*leaping up*). Momento! (*Taking a lump of sugar from his pocket and offering it to* SISTER THORN) A lump of sugar?

SISTER THORN (*with ill-concealed surprise*). No, thank you.

FRANKLIN (*going to the telephone*). The Lord has warned us off sugar! (*With a snigger*) Take salt! It's sweeter, and more spicy! . . . (*On the telephone*) Hello? . . . Hello? . . . Yes, that's right . . . Charlotte? Who's Charlotte? Never heard of her. Anyway, the master of the house is in conference. (*He hangs up.*)

ELVIRA. But, Franklin . . .

FRANKLIN (*returning it*). That must have been Charlotte.

ELVIRA (*half amused, half put-out*). But, Franklin, what about the Panicoffs?

FRANKLIN (*pompously*). The Panicoffs? Now there's a name to go to bed with! Never heard of them! (*In an aside to* ELVIRA) It's much more fun here. (*Settling himself down comfortably in front of* SISTER THORN) So you were saying, Sister Haw of the Holy Thorn . . .

SISTER THORN (*hurt*). Sister Thorn of the Holy Ghost.

FRANKLIN. I beg your pardon! . . . Darling, pour me another drink. (ELVIRA *fills the two glasses. They drink.* SISTER THORN, *still upright, appears to be gazing right through them. Putting down his glass*) . . . Sister, I find your conversation electrifying!

ELVIRA. Edifying!

FRANKLIN. To think we were going out into the world to indulge in futility, when here, in our own home . . . For us you are Providential.

SISTER THORN (*lowering her eyes*). I am just the instrument of Providence.

ELVIRA (*sensually*). And what a delicate instrument.

FRANKLIN (*determined to get full enjoyment out of the situation*). Sister Thorn, may I ask you a few questions?

SISTER THORN. Bleat away, Brother. And the Lord will shear your fleece.

FRANKLIN (*in a confidential tone*). Sister Thorn, since the inscrutable ways of the Lord led your parents to fornicate, as you say, in order to give you birth, so that we should one day have the pleasure of meeting you . . .

SISTER THORN.   Monsieur, you have drunk too much!

FRANKLIN.   Drunk too much . . . could that in your eyes be trans-
gression? Does not drink, my dear prickly Sister, flow through
many pages of the Holy Scriptures? Jesus Christ—and please let me
speak at last of the Son of God . . .

SISTER THORN (*wildly*).   Christ is our Saviour. Christ is our Ram.

FRANKLIN (*with the obstinate insistance of a drunkard*).   When, as I
was saying, Jesus Christ saw water, he saw red. At once he transformed
it into wine. Remember the wedding feast of Cana. And read the Old
Testament again: all those patriarchs with their shimmering beards,
dancing before the Ark, dead-drunk . . .

SISTER THORN (*shouting*).   Drunk with God, Monsieur! Drunk with
God!

FRANKLIN.   Drunk just the same.

ELVIRA (*bringing grist to her husband's mill*).   And what do you make
of Noah?

FRANKLIN.   Why yes, Noah.'Before me the Deluge.'

ELVIRA.   Noah, the drunkenness of Noah. That dear man succumbing
to the grapes from his vineyard and exposing his nakedness to his
two sons? Shem was the one who giggled, and Japheth the one who
blushed.

FRANKLIN.   Exactly. Shem and Japheth.

ELVIRA.   Am I inventing that? Isn't that attested, Sister, in the Holy
Book?

SISTER THORN (*standing up, with tears in her eyes*).   You're too
clever for me. I shall send you my Commanding Officer, Major Brompte

FRANKLIN.   No, no, don't get up! It would be such a shame if you left.
(*He makes her sit down again.*) We have no business with Major
Brompton. Confrontation with you is so positive, invigorating . . .

SISTER THORN.   You're two against one!

FRANKLIN.   But you, Sister Thorn of the Holy Ghost, all on your own,
you're Three in One. We're beaten from the start!

ELVIRA (*imitating* SISTER THORN, *insidiously*).   Go, lambkin, cast
yourself in the lion's mouth . . .

SISTER THORN (*as though whipped into action, suddenly rising and
singing in a loud, though still ferrety voice*).
> Into the mouth of the lion
> Little white ermine I go
> With nought but my faith to rely on
> Caught by surprise I lie low.
> With nought but my faith to rely on
> (*very softly*) Singing Matins, a good note to die on . . .
> Hosannah! Hosannah!
> I'm waving Heaven's banner.

ALL THREE.   Hosannah! Hosannah!
> Misericordia.

Like Popeye's spinach, this hymn has restored SISTER THORN's
vigour and magnified her zeal.

SISTER THORN (*vehemently*).   Noah! Yes indeed, let us speak of Noah.
   At that time abomination reigned throughout the world. Iniquity,
   thievery, sodomy, mesopotamy. All men were the children of Cain.
   So it came about that the Lord was sick at heart and wished to wipe
   out His creation once and for all, for His creation had become a
   nightmare unto Him.
FRANKLIN.   How fascinating!
SISTER THORN.   Be quiet. And He prepared Himself to send down a
   Flood, to bury the earth in a watery grave. But there was one just
   man: Noah. And the Lord, taking pity on him, took pity also on
   other men. And mankind was saved . . . But in our day where shall
   one just man be found? Who will turn away the anger of our Eternal
   Father? Who will ward off the destruction of our planet? . . . Time
   has run its course. When the wicked spring as the grass, they shall be
   forever exterminated.' Psalms, Chapter 92, Verse 9. 'Neither liars,
   thieves nor stockbrokers, fornicators nor transvestites, neither
   polluters, nor computers, philanderers nor customs officials shall
   inherit the kingdom of God.' Corinthians I, Chapter 6, Verse 9.
   (*With a touch of jubilation*) 'And the slain of Jehovah shall be
   counted in thousands even to the ends of the earth.' Jeremiah,
   Chapter 25, Verse 53.
ELVIRA.   Let's not get into a state, Sister Thorn. You're still here,
   home and dry . . .
SISTER THORN.   There won't even be time for the newborn babies
   to be born.
FRANKLIN.   I must say, if I shared your faith, rather than shout
   Noah's story from the rooftops, I'd hide it under a bushel . . .
   Because, so far as I can see, Thorniest of Sisters, the Lord made
   the same silly mistake all over again. He saved mankind, when it
   was thoroughly rotten, to put in its place a second version even more
   rotten than the first! If I were in His shoes, I'd be chewing my
   fingers with rage.
SISTER THORN (*quite crimson*).   God has no fingers, Monsieur. God
   has no feet. God has no stomach. God is not Who you think—or
   don't think— he is. So what the bloody hell! (*She bursts into tears.*)
ELVIRA.   Oh, come on now, don't start crying like a . . . like a . . .
FRANKLIN.   . . . like a thorn without a rose. (*The couple are enjoying
   themselves enormously.*)
SISTER THORN (*while choking back her tears, weakly*). Bloody hell.
ELVIRA.   My husband did at least express himself quite frankly.
FRANKLIN.   No offence meant.
SISTER THORN (*pulling a pamphlet from her briefcase and handing it
   to* FRANKLIN, *not without malice*).   Here, you just read that, *I*
   didn't write it. It's the word of the Lord our God. It only costs
   three francs, and in Belgium it's even cheaper.

ELVIRA.   Three francs for the word of the Lord our God, I think we
can just manage that.

FRANKLIN (*reading out the title, in great merriment*).   Hiya God!

SISTER THORN (*in confirmation, grimly*).   Hiya God!

FRANKLIN.   Has God gone American too?

SISTER THORN.   I'm not saying any more. Just you read it. (*She
sniffs and wipes away a tear.*)

FRANKLIN (*glancing through the pamphlet*).   June 17th. The Lord
addressed New Zealanders for seven hours on the race-course at
Alexandra Park, in Auckland . . .

SISTER THORN (*restored to confident pride*).   We printed twelve
million copies. We have Brothers and Sisters in the farthest reaches
of the globe.

ELVIRA.   Now isn't it good to know that there are still some
farthest reaches left . . . (*She pours herself out a drink.*)

SISTER THORN.   Just under a week ago, we converted a whole tribe of
Eskimos. They gave up hunting whales. Hallelujah!

ELVIRA.   Hallelujah! (*She empties her glass.*)

FRANKLIN (*to* SISTER THORN).   DU BON! DU BONNET!
DU BON DIEU is good for you! (*He drinks.*) And may one know why
the whale . . .

SISTER THORN.   Because those who seek the truth know that every
whale conceals a Jonah. And Jonah is the servant of Jehovah . . . should
one turn Jehovah's servant into whale-oil?

FRANKLIN.   I freely admit it would be very bad taste.

SISTER THORN (*exultant*).   Ephphatha! Ephphatha! Ah, Monsieur, read
and mark the word of the Lord. And your eyes shall open and your
knees shall bend and your ears shall ring and you shall become
acquainted with the Law . . . And the Law shall become dearer to you
than your eyes and your knees and your ears and . . . and . . . (*turning
to* ELVIRA) And your wife.

FRANKLIN (*clouding over*).   And my wife . . .

SISTER THORN.   Have you ever seriously considered murdering your
wife?

FRANKLIN (*with terrific conviction*).   *Have* I? You bet I have!

ELVIRA.   A cry from the heart.

FRANKLIN.   More than once! Twice!

SISTER THORN.   You poor unhappy man! You know not what you
say!

FRANKLIN.   Make no mistake, Sister. Never in all my life have I thought
about it as intently as at this moment.

SISTER THORN (*hoping for comfort from* ELVIRA).   But you, Madame,
you the sacrificial victim, you seem to . . .

ELVIRA.   The same goes for me, Sister. It's just the same for me.
(*Aiming at her husband*) Bang, bang, bang . . . (FRANKLIN *crumples
up.*) One's just got to keep going.

FRANKLIN AND ELVIRA.
Thirteen years of conjugal bliss
But where are the Bengal lights I miss?!

SISTER THORN. Oh the posterity of Abraham
    Bearded children of their dam
    Comfort this poor bleating lamb!
FRANKLIN. You really won't be tempted by this armchair?
    (*Lasciviously*) . . . Stretch your legs out a bit, give your bosom
    more breathing space . . .
SISTER THORN. I might have known it! I should have been on
    my guard! You are two of Satan's hell-hounds. Beelzebub's. Two
    of the fiends of Balaam, of Zebulon, of Phiphiboseth! . . . But you
    don't scare me, the two of you. 'To the children of light Jahweh
    offers the shield of light'. Genesis, Chapter 4, Verse 26. And just
    to prove that you don't frighten me. (SISTER THORN *gets up and
    defiantly clamps herself in the large armchair.*)
FRANKLIN. Gosh you are . . .
ELVIRA. Joshua!

*The couple are growing visibly more and more excited by the abnormal
development of the situation — at the poor girl's expense.*

SISTER THORN. The unbelievable makes welcome the believer. He
    shall be neither burned by the fire nor lashed by the wind nor made
    wet by the water. Drink! (*She seizes* FRANKLIN's *empty glass and
    holds it out to him commandingly.*)
FRANKLIN. A drink! But . . . at your service, General Thorn, at your
    service . . . Gin? Whisky?
SISTER THORN (*resolutely*). Vodka.
ELVIRA (*half-drunk, hurrying to pour her out a whopping great
    glassful of vodka*). It's straight from the Dead Sea.
SISTER THORN (*after drinking it down in one, without turning a hair*).
    'And the lions fell upon the martyrs packed in the arena. And oh!
    Wonder of wonders! They tenderly laid their heads upon the womens'
    breasts and licked the faces of the men.' Daniel, Chapter 3, Verse 15 . . .
    (*scornfully*) Small beer, your spirits. Small beer!
FRANKLIN. Small beer! Small beer!
ELVIRA (*as though about to tell a secret*). Sister Scorn of the Holy
    Ghost . . .
SISTER THORN (*rectifying*). Thorn.
ELVIRA. Thorn. Your zeal, your Faith, your fearlessness encourage me
    to open my heart to you and make a confession. Yes, to confess
    myself to you.
FRANKLIN. Dreadful thought!

SISTER THORN *holds her empty glass out to* FRANKLIN *without a
word. He fills it at once.*

ELVIRA. To what depths can human turpitude descend? Have you any
    true idea of that, Sister? And didn't the good Lord send you here to
    go down into the pit and find out? (*As she swallows a mouthful of
    vodka* SISTER THORN *cannot repress a shiver.*) . . . My husband

and I . . . it's all far worse than you think . . . It's only too true that we hate each other, that we each harbour murderous thoughts about the other.

SISTER THORN (*joyously*).   Hallelujah!

ELVIRA.   Even early on, soon after we met, my husband was after my life.

FRANKLIN (*coming back into the game*).   And she was after mine. She omits that minor detail!

ELVIRA.   And it's been going on now for thirteen years. And during those thirteen years it's been a constant battle to know which of the two is going to get the mortal blow in first!

FRANKLIN.   Like those Western films, you know? The one who's quickest on the draw . . .

ELVIRA.   . . . or who's left-handed . . .

FRANKLIN.   Or has a black patch over one eye. Fantastic.

ELVIRA.   So we're worn to a shadow.

FRANKLIN.   Two shadows, always on the qui-vive, spying on each other . . .

ELVIRA.   . . . keeping our eyes open for the slightest movement from the other one: Enemy Number One!

FRANKLIN.   Yes, night and day we're on the watch, Sister. Beneath our blankets, between our sheets, in the bathroom, at breakfast, in the glory hole, in the lift . . .

ELVIRA.   It's frightful! Especially in the loo!

SISTER THORN.   Hallelujah! (*She drinks.*)

FRANKLIN.   It's a good thing we haven't a cellar.

ELVIRA.   We live in a permanent state of terror.

FRANKLIN.   Has she put arsenic in my plum pudding?

ELVIRA.   One morning, my bra started giving me terrible burns.

FRANKLIN.   Did she step up the voltage of my electric razor?

ELVIRA.   Walk backwards, Elvira—my name is Elvira—if you turn your back he'll leap at you, and knock you down with a feather.

FRANKLIN.   Look out for that shiny step, Franklin. She's smeared it with peanut butter again . . .

ELVIRA.   And that clear soup which suddenly rolled into a ball inside my stomach? (*Miming the scene*) Give me some air! Help! Air! Air!

FRANKLIN.   And my car radio? I was alone in the car, coasting along at seventy, when the newscaster suddenly announced my death!
(*A pause. Both of them seem to have run out of inspiration.* SISTER THORN, *with a glazed expression on her face, is finishing her glass of vodka.*)

ELVIRA.   How was it, when things were like that, that we were ever able to have children? And why?

FRANKLIN.   Yes, why?

ELVIRA (*savouring her own invention*).   So they could serve as hostages.

FRANKLIN.   That's it: hostages! I managed to take her little boy prisoner.

ELVIRA.   And I confined his little girl to her room.

FRANKLIN.   One word out of place and I plug Pascal into the power-point. Elvira can't bear it when Pascal screams.

ELVIRA.   One dirty look and I plunge Véronique's head for minutes on end in a basin of Vichy water. Franklin can't bear it when Véronique keeps quiet.

FRANKLIN.   The balance of terror!

SISTER THORN (*suddenly, in a little girl's voice*).   But it's sheer Hell!

FRANKLIN.   It is sheer Hell, Sister Horn of the Holy Roast. It's Hell all right!

SISTER THORN *pours herself out a drink, then stands up and takes a few steps with her glass in her hand, slightly staggering.*

SISTER THORN (*in accents of joy*).   Hell!

Hysterical giggle. She paces up and down the room, tentatively examining each object.

FRANKLIN.   There's nothing more commonplace than Hell: four walls, a few bits of furniture, two or three abstract paintings, an old carpet and a telly ... And in that little concentration cell, couple after couple of married couples ... Men and women, couples galore. Husbands and wives, think of their lives, Darbys and Joans, husbands like stones, wives like old bones ...

ELVIRA.   Franklin, you're overdoing it!

FRANKLIN (*fully launched and driving* SISTER THORN *into a corner*). For there are thousands and thousands of couples like us, locked in the drab routine of boredom, masticating the hours like chewing gum, threatened with eternal invitations from the Panicoffs, thousands of Panicoffs who don't even know they *are* Panicoffs and will never be anything else. Matthew, Chapter 4, Verse 28 ... And in this desert, in this vast over-populated desert ... (*The phone bell cuts him short.* ELVIRA *rushes to the telephone*.) No, don't pick it up! For God's sake don't pick it up! How can the damned help the damned? (*The bell goes on ringing.*) That bell is tolling for the dead. And the living dead! ... Has God ever phoned you, Sister Thorn?

SISTER THORN (*surrendering to the alcohol and the general atmosphere, in a failing voice*).   It's hot! It's very hot! (*She takes off her hat, and gives it to* FRANKLIN.)

FRANKLIN.   Thanks.

SISTER THORN.   Hot.

FRANKLIN.   It's a question of habit, Sister. Hell's that too, you know: all a question of habit.

ELVIRA.   We can't regulate the heating.

SISTER THORN (*distracted*).   No, of course, in Hell ...

FRANKLIN.   Simmering between floor and ceiling. Stewing in our own juice.

SISTER THORN (*raising her glass*).   Cheers!

ELVIRA AND FRANKLIN (*raising their glasses*). Cheers!

SISTER THORN, *having put her glass down again, takes off her jacket and like a sleepwalker hands it to* FRANKLIN, *who is still holding her hat.*

FRANKLIN. Thanks.

SISTER THORN (*looks at herself in the mirror*). Major Brompton has
   forbidden us to look in the glass. (*Hysterical giggle.*) I've a funny sort
   of face. Don't you think I've a funny sort of face? All puffed up
   inside.

ELVIRA. You ought to drop your hair onto your shoulders . . . May I?

ELVIRA *undoes her hair.* SISTER THORN *is docile and lets her do it.*

* *

This at least is what will happen if the actress is naturally endowed with beautiful long hair.

Alternatively ELVIRA *can place a wig on her head.*

The alternative version will go as follows:

SISTER THORN. Major Brompton has forbidden us to look in the glass.
   (*Hysterical giggle.*) I've a funny sort of face. Don't you think I've a
   funny sort of face? All puffed up inside.

ELVIRA. You can change it if you like. Fine feathers make fine birds!
   Here, why don't you put this wig on?

To the great amusement of FRANKLIN *she picks her wig up from the dressing-table.*

SISTER THORN. Oh! A wig! Just like Louis the Fourteenth!

ELVIRA. Perhaps not quite! (*She puts her wig on* SISTER THORN.)

SISTER THORN (*quite drunk and gazing delightedly at her reflection
   in the mirror*). I look like someone who looks a bit like me,
   someone I don't really know . . .

ELVIRA *puts lipstick on her mouth.* SISTER THORN *is docile and lets it happen, with a kind of 'secret pleasure'. Then* ELVIRA *displays the now transformed* SISTER THORN *to her husband.*

* *

ELVIRA. (*contemplating her handiwork with satisfaction*). There . . .

FRANKLIN. Oh! You're much prettier like that!

ELVIRA (*sensually*). You're very pretty indeed, Sister Thorn!

FRANKLIN. My Sister, if you weren't my Sister . . .

SISTER THORN (*in a more and more trance-like state*). The wolf shall
   dwell with the lamb and the leopard shall lie down with the kid. And

the lion shall eat straw like the ox . . . (*She empties her glass of vodka.*) . . . And the suckling child shall play by the viper's den. And the weaned child put his hand in the basilisk's cave . . . And they shall not hurt nor destroy. Isaiah, Chapter 11, Verses 7, 8 and 9. (*She undoes her blouse.*)

ELVIRA.   You're going to take off your blouse!

FRANKLIN (*enchanted by this stroke of luck*).   Take off anything you like, cast off, Brother! Cast away: St. Mark, St. Luke, St. Paul and St. Chrysostom . . .

SISTER THORN *mechanically hands her blouse to* ELVIRA *who gives it to* FRANKLIN.

ELVIRA (*in a low voice to* FRANKLIN).   Chauvinist Pig!

FRANKLIN (*in a low voice to* ELVIRA).   Lesbian!

SISTER THORN *slips down the shoulder straps of her petticoat. She is wearing a black bra.*

SISTER THORN (*ecstatically*).   Sister Thorn of the Holy Ghost of the Black Brassière. That's the name the Lord gives me in secret. That's the way He sees me!

ELVIRA.   The Lord's got second sight!

FRANKLIN.   Somehow it reminds me of New Zealand: perhaps it's the All Blacks. No connection.

SISTER THORN.   I shall break your haughty pride. Your rump shall be my foot-stool. Your shattered bones my trumpet.

FRANKLIN.   I bet that's Ezekiel!

SISTER THORN.   Ezekiel, Chapter 29, Verses 8 and 9.

ELVIRA.   Your language, in fact, is in code: all figures of speech . . .

FRANKLIN.   Jesus Christ was like everyone else. He could never express Himself simply. He talked in parables.

SISTER THORN (*who is not listening to them*).   The Lord sent His Son down to earth, clad only in a linen robe, a robe of light. But men have been blinded by that light.

FRANKLIN.   It's true you can hardly say mankind . . .

SISTER THORN (*coming down to earth*).   Poor mankind! . . . When I walk through the street buttoned up to the throat: 'Strip! Strip!' I hear them shouting as I pass. Strip.

FRANKLIN.   Vox populi, vox dei!

SISTER THORN (*shouting*).   Strip!

ELVIRA.   Don't shout like that, Sister. You'll wake the children!

SISTER THORN.   Even if they don't shout it through their mouths, they shout it through their eyes, through their hands, through their noses: Strip!

ELVIRA.   You're not in the street right now!

SISTER THORN.   The whole of the Western World has returned to the anal phase. That's what Major Brompton says!

FRANKLIN (*getting more and more excited, he puts on* SISTER

THORN's *hat, which was getting in his way, and holds out his glass*).
Whisky, Sister Elvira!

ELVIRA (*removing the bottle*).   You're tight already!

SISTER THORN (*more and more disturbing*).   I frighten you, don't I?
I frighten you? . . . The children of Cain tremble and gnash their
teeth and are glutted with themselves, so falling into anguish and
despair . . . (*Illuminated*) But the children of Abel live in joy, love
and long-suffering, goodness, faith, gentleness and self-discipline.
Galatians, Chapter 5, Verses 22 and 23. Self-control . . . (SISTER
THORN *adroitly drops her skirt to the floor, revealing brightly
coloured, ridiculously long Bermuda shorts*) Sister Thorn of the Holy
Ghost of Bermuda, that's the name the Lord gives me in secret, that's
the way He sees me now!

ELVIRA *has picked up the skirt and mechanically passed it to*
FRANKLIN.

FRANKLIN (*in admiration before* SISTER THORN).   Praised be the
secrets of the Lord!

SISTER THORN.   Strip! Strip! . . . Away with this monotony, this
emptiness, this gloom!

FRANKLIN.   Personally . . .

ELVIRA.   Shut up, Franklin!

SISTER THORN.   But the Lord is not gloomy: he created the giraffe! . . .
And I'm not gloomy either — even here in this Hell of yours. And I
can see you, more naked than a skeleton's bones, I can see exactly
what you are: a couple of wrecks.

FRANKLIN.   Now you're going too far!

SISTER THORN.   A couple of fossils. And you don't know what to do with
your lives, your life's like an old blanket, too thin to keep a beggar
warm, with the cold creeping in through its mothholes. (*She starts
making for the bottle of vodka, but* ELVIRA *stands in the way.*)

ELVIRA.   You've had enough of that 'small beer'.

FRANKLIN (*to* ELVIRA).   Spoil-sport!

SISTER THORN.   Truth frightens you. You're frightened of the truth!
(*She unhooks her Bermudas.*)

ELVIRA.   What are you doing now?

SISTER THORN (*like a virgin preparing herself for the joy of
martyrdom*).   Saint Blandine removed her clothes, and when she was
quite nude, snow fell all over the kingdom . . . (*The Bermudas fall to her
feet, revealing black panties with a rose embroidered on one side.*)

ELVIRA (*preventing her from undressing completely*).   Now look, you
didn't come here to do a strip-tease! What a way to go on!

ELVIRA *catches hold of* SISTER THORN's *hands, while the latter
struggles.*

SISTER THORN.   Why don't you leave me alone!

ELVIRA.   You're not Saint Blandine and what's more it's summertime.
Get dressed!

FRANKLIN (*disappointed by* ELVIRA'*s attitude*).   Come off it,
   Elvira! If Sister Thorn of the Holy Stark Naked Ghost . . .
ELVIRA.   Shut up, you dirty old man and pass me all that. You look
   like a scarecrow. (*She snatches* SISTER THORN'*s clothes away from
   him, except the hat, which he's still wearing on his head, and throws
   them to the* SISTER.) Here, hurry up!
SISTER THORN.   There's no hurry in Hell! . . . (*Hysterical giggle.*)
FRANKLIN (*furiously*).   My wife has no respect for the rules. Please,
   Sister, please . . .
ELVIRA.   Kindly pay no attention to my husband. Come on now,
   get dressed!
SISTER THORN.   In my own good time! (*Shouting and almost weeping*)
   Just now I want to strip!

ELVIRA *delivers her a resounding slap. All three are stupefied.*
A moment of silence.
The slap has its effect, however, and SISTER THORN *obeys. She gets
dressed again, without saying a word, tearful, embarrassed and ashamed.*

FRANKLIN.   You struck my Sister! . . . You struck our Sister!
ELVIRA.   There's only one cure for hysterics. This comedy's lasted long
   enough.
FRANKLIN.   Elvira, I hardly recognise you. What's got into you?
ELVIRA (*holding out* SISTER THORN'*s jacket to her, coldly*).   Your
   jacket.
FRANKLIN.   And we were just getting somewhere, for once . . . (SISTER
   THORN *conscientiously buttons up her jacket.*)   Sister Thorn of the
   Blessed Slap, now you can guess what I have to put up with in private . . .
   'Thirteen years of conjugal bliss'.
ELVIRA (*in a low voice*).   For God's sake, Franklin!
SISTER THORN.   Blessed are the humbled . . . Blessed the dishevelled.
   (*She is tidying her hair.*) Blessed are those who suffer persecution.
   (*Suddenly pointing*) Oh, look! Over there in the corner . . . Can't you
   see? (FRANKLIN *and* ELVIRA *stare in vain, they can see nothing.*)
   An egg. An egg as big as a bell. All on fire. With the feet of an ostrich!
FRANKLIN (*in a low voice*).   Off her rocker!
ELVIRA.   It's not a bad performance.
FRANKLIN.   You really think so?
SISTER THORN (*apostrophizing the invisible monster*).   Away with you,
   silly little bugger! (*Appearing to be watching it go*) See! It's gone. Piping
   hot, right up through the ceiling. Didn't like me calling it a bugger.
ELVIRA (*calmly but firmly, as she might talk to a mental patient, taking
   care not to alarm her*).   Right. Good. Excellent. Bravo.
   Congratulations . . . Now you're all dressed, you look like your old
   self again, and your legs are back to normal . . . (*To* FRANKLIN)
   Franklin, Sister's hat . . .
FRANKLIN (*forgetting he is still wearing it on his head*).   Hat?

ELVIRA *takes the hat off* FRANKLIN's *head and puts it on*
SISTER THORN's.

ELVIRA.   There. Perfect. Equipped from top to toe. Now it's your
turn to fly away, Sister, but in a sensible way, through the door.
SISTER THORN.   Pity, your Hell was nice and cosy. You gave me such
a warm welcome: Come in! come in, Mademoiselle! Would you like
tea? Or chocolate? Would you like us to tuck you up in a great big
white bed? (*She takes a few steps, swaying slightly, towards the
telephone.*)
ELVIRA.   Are you all right to go home alone?
SISTER THORN.   I am never alone. Jehovah inhabits my spine, my
womb, even the tips of my fingers.
FRANKLIN.   Jehovah doesn't waste any time!
SISTER THORN (*at the telephone*).   I'm going to make a call.
ELVIRA.   You're going to make a call?
SISTER THORN.   Yes, I'm going to call up Major Brompton. The
Kingdom of God is nigh, Major Brompton, the Kingdom of God is
nigh! Armageddon. Big bang! (*She picks up the receiver.*)
ELVIRA (*taking the phone from her and hanging up*).   Leave Major
Brompton in peace. I'll call a taxi. In the state you're in!
SISTER THORN.   A taxi!
ELVIRA.   I'll give you the money. Where do you live?
SISTER THORN.   At Major Brompton's . . . in Montmartre.
FRANKLIN.   Major Brompton! Major Brompton! . . .
SISTER THORN (*rather sweetly*).   I often dream I'm carrying a
revolver with me. And whenever I meet one of Jehovah's enemies,
I take it out and shoot him. Then I call up Major Brompton —
another one gone! The Kingdom of God is nigh! The Kingdom of
God is nigh!
FRANKLIN (*jumping with pleasure*).   That would make a terrific
ending: the two of us shot by Sister Thorn of the Holy Ghost, laid
out there on the carpet, stone dead, another two of Jehovah's
enemies gone . . .
SISTER THORN (*clapping her hands*).   Oh yes!
FRANKLIN.   . . . then Pascal and Véronique woken up by the shots
and bursting in in their nightshirts: 'What a pretty baby-sitter!' And
Sister Thorn of the Blessed thirty-five-millimetre-small-bore Holy
Ghost, falling on her knees in front of the two orphans . . .
(*He falls on his knees*) 'Oh the little Cherubs! Oh, the darling little
Cherubims!' (*Standing up again, exhausted.*) Curtain.
ELVIRA.   Franklin, you're a pain in the neck, you make me sick!
SISTER THORN.   Oh yes, the two orphans, the two little martyrs . . .
Where are they?
ELVIRA (*her exasperation no longer under control*).   Now, Miss, we've
had enough of you and your ravings. Finish! And as you're big
enough to go home alone, go and convert Jehovah's enemies

elsewhere! (SISTER THORN *totters and falls on* ELVIRA.)

SISTER THORN. All right, all right. Don't push me. I understand, I'm off.

ELVIRA. Not that way, that's the children's bedroom. This way. (*She takes her by the shoulders*.)

SISTER THORN. All right, all right. Don't panic me!

FRANKLIN. What did I tell you? A tigress.

SISTER THORN. I understand . . . there's a time to drop in and a time to clock out. Ecclesiastes, Chapter 5, Verse 33. (*She starts to disappear*) Good-bye, Monsieur. I'm sure Jehovah will catch up with you!

FRANKLIN. I'm afraid he will! Bye-bye, Sister Thorn! My regards to the Major. (*Suddenly discovering* SISTER THORN's *briefcase at the foot of the armchair*) Hey! Forgot your briefcase!

SISTER THORN. Ah yes, my briefcase.

FRANKLIN. Hi, God! . . . Don't move, I'll chuck it over. (*He is slinging the briefcase, about to throw it, when a revolver falls out.*)

SISTER THORN (*quite naturally*). Oh, my revolver!

FRANKLIN. Good Lord, a revolver!

ELVIRA. A revolver.

SISTER THORN. My revolver.

ELVIRA. Her revolver.

FRANKLIN. A revolver . . . Now then, little Sister, just tell me . . .

SISTER THORN. Give me back my revolver.

FRANKLIN. One moment! (*He examines the weapon attentively*.)

ELVIRA. Franklin, do you realize? . . . And you trot around with a revolver in your briefcase! Are you out of your mind!

SISTER THORN. Don't insult me, Madame.

FRANKLIN (*breaks into a peal of disturbing laughter. Suddenly aiming at his wife*). Hands up, Elvira!

SISTER THORN. Be careful! It's loaded!

FRANKLIN. And you, Thorny Ghost, don't move!

ELVIRA. For God's sake, Franklin, this is no time to play the fool!

FRANKLIN (*continuing to aim at* ELVIRA). Thanks to you, Sister, the situation's suddenly turned in my favour . . . I told you, didn't I, that with us, it's like being in one of those Westerns . . . At this particular moment, I wouldn't be in your shoes, Elvira! Your life doesn't count for much now! Hands up!

ELVIRA *who naturally ignores the command, does however try to get out of the line of fire.*

ELVIRA. Franklin, stop it!

FRANKLIN. First, in the presence of a witness, you'll say you're sorry for all you've put me through in thirteen years.

ELVIRA. You've had too much to drink, Franklin. For God's sake, stop it!

FRANKLIN. Say you're sorry, or I fire.

SISTER THORN. Oh dear, oh dear!

FRANKLIN. Tell your little husband you're sorry you turned him into a little husband, a little civil servant, a little creepy-crawly thing . . .

ELVIRA. Franklin, please stop this little game. It's in very bad taste!

FRANKLIN.(*following her around*). A little Prince Consort . . . a little Swiss gnome . . .

SISTER THORN. Oh dear, oh dear!

ELVIRA. You're completely stoned!

FRANKLIN. I'm counting up to three . . . One . . . I'm sorry, little husband . . . Two . . . Three!! (*He fires. The sharp click of a child's revolver, while at the same time* SISTER THORN *utters a shriek.* ELVIRA *has collapsed into the armchair. A brief moment of silence.* FRANKLIN *bursts out laughing and blows into the tip of the barrel of the revolver, which is smoking slightly.*) A miracle! She's still alive! (ELVIRA, *in her armchair, suddenly starts sobbing, in a kind of nervous collapse.* FRANKLIN, *thunderstruck*) It was a joke, darling! Look! You can see it's only a toy.

ELVIRA.(*between sobs*). You're so stupid! So stupid! (*Her sobbing redoubles.*)

FRANKLIN (*kneeling in front of* ELVIRA). A child's revolver! You see . . . I got carried away in the heat of the moment. It was all a joke! I never imagined . . .

SISTER THORN. It's a funny sort of joke . . .

ELVIRA (*in a kind of gasp*). Get her out of here.

FRANKLIN (*standing up*). And you, Spiky, we've seen enough of you. Buzz off!

SISTER THORN. My revolver.

FRANKLIN. I'll give this little plaything to Pascal, in memory of you. Scram!

SISTER THORN. But . . .

FRANKLIN. But what?

SISTER THORN. Nothing, nothing. Anyone would think you were abnormal.

FRANKLIN. I wonder . . . The door's over there on the right.

SISTER THORN (*as she goes*). I'll tell Major Brompton. I'll tell Major Brompton . . . Antichrist! (*She vanishes, slamming the door behind her.*)

ELVIRA (*still shaken with sobs*). You're so stupid! You're . . .

FRANKLIN (*kneeling in front of* ELVIRA). Forgive me, Elvira . . . Please forgive me . . . I could never have guessed all this would upset you so! . . . Come on, Elvira, cheer up . . . I'm here. She's gone. (*Aside*) I won't forget *that* baby-sitter! (ELVIRA *is trying to get her breath.* FRANKLIN, *more and more anxious*) . . . Can't you breathe? You want me to open the window? . . . Don't you feel well, Elvira? (*He taps her hands and cheeks.*) . . . Do you want me to call Doctor Cameroun?

ELVIRA (*still catching her breath*). No, no, don't move. It'll pass.

FRANKLIN. Darling, you didn't take all that nonsense seriously?
Perhaps I did play my part a bit too well . . . (*Trying to calm her*)
And so did you, you weren't at all bad just now . . . when you
invented that stuff about hell and the way we tortured our
children . . .

ELVIRA (*straightening up*). Did you hear that cry? Pascal or
Véronique? Sshh! . . . (*A short moment of silence.*)

FRANKLIN. Peace and quiet. Once they've gone to sleep, you know
very well the whole Seventh Fleet could bombard us . . . (*A fresh fit
of sobbing.*) Elvira, you're not going to start again! . . . We're both at
fault, the two of us, and that's a fact . . . We went much too far with
that poor crazy girl. Much too far. And it's a good thing you threw in
your hand! (*More sobs from* ELVIRA.) I must say, with all that
interminable waiting — and on an empty stomach too! — you and I
were both at the end of our tether . . . And with the booze on top of
that! . . . Elvira, say something!

ELVIRA (*as though hallucinating*). Oh! Look! Over there in the
corner? . . . Can't you see? . . . A corpse!

FRANKLIN (*in consternation*). Now look here, Elvira . . .

ELVIRA. The corpse of our love. Magnificent! A beautiful corpse.
(*Her sobbing redoubles.*)

FRANKLIN (*severely*). Now *please*, Elvira, don't *you* start acting up!

ELVIRA. There's not enough air, I can't breathe.

FRANKLIN. Is there really something wrong? . . . Shall I go and look in
our medicine chest to see if there's any . . .

ELVIRA (*still trying to breathe properly*). You know very well,
Franklin, there really *is* something wrong . . . There's something
wrong with me. And there's something wrong with you . . . We're a
couple of fossils!

FRANKLIN. You sound like that crazy girl! She's completely under-
mined you, that Holy Ghostly little mouse!

ELVIRA (*in a sort of outburst*). Franklin, we used to love each other!
How we used to love each other!

FRANKLIN (*bringing up another chair*). Put your legs up, and you'll
feel better. (*She puts her legs up.* FRANKLIN *stuffs a cushion behind
her back.*)

ELVIRA. What's gone wrong, Franklin? How did we ever get like this?
Boring each other. Avoiding each other. Going out to dine with the
Panicoffs!

FRANKLIN (*stroking her hair*). Never mind, sweetheart, it's all right . . .
We're not going to dinner with the Panicoffs.

ELVIRA (*her face suddenly lighting up*). It's ages since you called me
'sweetheart'! . . . Oh, Franklin, the good times we used to have!
Such *fun!* We were so happy we never even noticed!

FRANKLIN. Life's so stupid. It gets more and more complex, more
bitty, more twitchy . . .

ELVIRA. But that's just it! If even *we* can't manage to get on
together, to love each other, to . . . form a rampart . . .

FRANKLIN. The human couple: the greatest adventure of modern
times!

ELVIRA. Please don't joke about it. Do you remember? You used to
say to me: The important thing is the present, the presence of what
is present. The present is a gift.

FRANKLIN. How can the present survive? Men are such misers today
Even their more generous and revolutionary ideas become a pretext
for inflating their precious little egos.

ELVIRA. Now you're talking the way you used to ... . Oh, Franklin,
I love you! (*She throws herself into his arms. They lovingly
embrace.*)

FRANKLIN. Do you remember? You used to say that so often, I
had to start fining you. That's how I bought my photographic
gear . . . All those cameras that disappeared!

ELVIRA. Don't you think that, as photographs go, Véronique and
Pascal turned out pretty well?

FRANKLIN. Yes, Elvira. They developed very nicely. I ought to
consult the book of rules again! (*The telephone rings.*) Let the
Panicoffs bury the Panicoffs. Luke, Chapter 26, Verse 3.

ELVIRA. Franklin, I always had faith in you. I always shall: 'From
Eternity to Eternity.' Jeremiah, Chapter 7, Verse 7.

FRANKLIN. And you are again for me: 'the flesh of my spirit and the
spirit of my flesh.' (*As he might say the word* 'Colossal') Colossians,
Chapter 5, Verse 77. (*The telephone is still ringing. They kiss.*) . . .
You're so beautiful, darling, so beautiful! Your eyes are like doves.
Your teeth a flock of ewe-lambs . . . Your two breasts . . .

The set collapses.
The glow of a great blaze. Explosions. Sounds of machine-gun fire.
The voice of SISTER THORN, *tremendously amplified:* The Kingdom
of God is nigh! The Kingdom of God is nigh!
The sounds of a fanatical crowd rejoicing.
Piercing sobs and cries from Pascal and Véronique. Explosions.
Shattering chords from an organ.
And again: The Kingdom of God is nigh! The Kingdom of God is nigh!
Very brief fragments of pop music. Explosions.
While this is going on, FRANKLIN *has pulled down the zip of* ELVIRA
*dress and revealed her naked shoulders. They stay there silently, clinging
to each other, lovingly, at the centre of this apocalyptic scene.*
Silence.

VOICE (*impersonal, off*). 'And male and female together shall be as
fragile as death itself, and as enduring as hope.' Obadiah, Chapter 7,
Verse 25.

Gradual blackout.

CURTAIN

THE JELLYFISHES' BANQUET

A Play for Radio

Characters

PSYCHOANALYST
SHE